ACTION THEORY AND SOCIAL SCIENCE

SYNTHESE LIBRARY

MONOGRAPHS ON EPISTEMOLOGY,

LOGIC, METHODOLOGY, PHILOSOPHY OF SCIENCE,

SOCIOLOGY OF SCIENCE AND OF KNOWLEDGE,

AND ON THE MATHEMATICAL METHODS OF

SOCIAL AND BEHAVIORAL SCIENCES

Managing Editor:

JAAKKO HINTIKKA, *Academy of Finland and Stanford University*

Editors:

ROBERT S. COHEN, *Boston University*

DONALD DAVIDSON, *University of Chicago*

GABRIËL NUCHELMANS, *University of Leyden*

WESLEY C. SALMON, *University of Arizona*

VOLUME 120

INGMAR PÖRN

ACTION THEORY
AND SOCIAL SCIENCE

Some Formal Models

D. REIDEL PUBLISHING COMPANY

DORDRECHT-HOLLAND / BOSTON-U.S.A.

Library of Congress Cataloging in Publication Data

Pörn, Ingmar.
    Action theory and social science.

    (Synthese library; v. 120)
    Bibliography: p.
    Includes index.
    1. Social sciences—Methodology. 2. Act (Philosophy)
3. Cybernetics. I. Title.
H62.P57   301'.01'8   77—12391
ISBN 90—277—0846—0

Published by D. Reidel Publishing Company,
P.O. Box 17, Dordrecht, Holland

Sold and distributed in the U.S.A., Canada, and Mexico
by D. Reidel Publishing Company, Inc.
Lincoln Building, 160 Old Derby Street, Hingham,
Mass. 02043, U.S.A.

Printed in The Netherlands

TABLE OF CONTENTS

PREFACE

This book is intended as a contribution to the foundations of the sciences of man, especially the social sciences. It has been argued with increasing frequency in recent years that the vocabulary of social science is to a large extent an action vocabulary and that any attempt to systematize concepts and establish bases for understanding in the field cannot, therefore, succeed unless it is firmly built on action theory. I think that these claims are substantially correct, but at the same time it seems to me that action theory, as it is relevant to social science, still awaits vital contributions from logic and philosophy. For example, it has often been said, rightly I believe, that situations in which two or more agents interact constitute the subject-matter of social science. But have we got an action theory which is rich enough or comprehensive enough to allow us to characterize the interaction situation? I think not. Once we have such a theory, however, we should be able to give an accurate account of central social phenomena and to articulate our conceptions about the nature of social reality.

The conceptual scheme advanced in this book consists, in the first instance, of solutions to a number of characterization problems, i.e. problems which may be expressed by questions of the form "What is the nature of ...?" and which require for their solutions the precise characterization of a class or a concept. Problems of this sort abound in philosophy and those that are attempted here include: What is the nature of an act, activity, and proceeding? What is an intention? What is it to act intentionally? What is influence? What is the nature of interaction? What is a social system?

The conceptual scheme generates, and it is reasonable to demand that it should generate, questions about the relations between the categories concerned. Questions of this sort may or may not be decidable *a priori*, in the light of the solutions to the characterization problems. For example, it surely is the case that if an agent acts in order to do something else, he does what he does intentionally. By contrast, the question of the nature of the relation between intention and action in intentional action is a more speculative matter.

In the early stages of the enterprise the time-varying (dynamic) aspects of human action receive little attention. It would be a mistake, however, to think that a theory of action could be comprehensive without dealing with

situations that change with time. In my attempt to treat this aspect I use the
basic tool of cybernetics, the notion of an information-feedback control
loop. In the concluding chapter the main results of the work inform some
topical issues concerning the explanation and understanding of human
action.

It may be said, quite generally, that it has been my concern to bring
together various theoretical approaches to social reality. My orientation in
this respect is of course based on the assumption that illumination of
problems of interest is to be found in a number of specialized disciplines. I
find it a challenging and worthwhile task to try to map out a middle way
between the detailed construction of theories in social science and the
philosopher's concern for the general case.

It will become evident that a large-scale or high-level theoretical attitude
dominates much of my detailed work. This is the conception of man as agent.
According to it, the human individual is an acting creature, i.e. a being
capable of taking or initiating action; and, secondly, a reacting creature, i.e.
a being capable of acting in the light of his knowledge of circumstances and
of the requirements made of the circumstances by the ends set by him. This
conception does not receive much attention as such. The reason is that I
think it is best established by implication and accretion of points and views
on diverse topics and themes.

I would like to express my gratitude to Professor Stig Kanger for his
encouragement and constructive intellectual support, and to Dr. Lars Lindahl,
Dr. Lennart Nordenfelt, and Docent Sören Stenlund for helpful criticism. I
am also most grateful to my colleague Mr. A. J. I. Jones, whose observations
and comments have provided me with a test ground for many of the devices
employed in this book; the final typescript also benefited from his advice and
that of Mr. P. Morris. Finally, many thanks are due to my friend and com-
panion Mrs. Margaret Cooper for her patience with me while writing the book.

I dedicate the book to my mother and to the memory of my father.

University of Birmingham   I.P.
March 1977

CHAPTER 1

ACTION MODALITIES

In this chapter we lay the foundation of our action theory. Extensions and elaborations of the theory will be given in subsequent chapters. As for methodology, we proceed by defining a logically well-written language. This is made comprehensive enough to serve as a general frame of our inquiry into not only action concepts but also a number of other concepts which soon arise in any fuller discussion of matters concerning action. We make the language serve as such a frame by using it to formulate definitions, classifications, and propositions (if not theories properly so called) in terms of which a volume of intuitive material can be marshalled and understood.

1. SOME REMARKS ON THE LANGUAGE L

The language $L(Pr, X, Mo)$ or L, for short, is determined by a set Pr of predicate letters or expressions, a set X of individual constants, and a set Mo of symbols for modalities. L employs the symbols that determine it and in addition symbols of the following categories: individual variables; the symbols $\sim$, &, ∨, ⊃, and ≡ called respectively the negation sign, the conjunction sign, the disjunction sign, the (material) implication sign, and the (material) equivalence sign; the symbols ∀ and ∃ called respectively the universal and the existential quantifier; and, finally, punctuation symbols.

The class of well-formed formulas or wffs of L is defined inductively in the same way as the class of wffs of (languages of) modal predicate logic. Thus any finite sequence of symbols of L, i.e. any finite collection of symbols occurring in order, is a wff of L if and only if it is of one of the following forms:

1. $P(a_1, a_2, ..., a_k)$ where P is a k-place predicate letter and $(a_1, a_2, ..., a_k)$ is a sequence of symbols such that a_i ($i = 1, 2, ..., k$) is either an individual variable or an individual constant;
2. $\sim p$, $(p$ & $q)$, $(p \vee q)$, $(p \supset q)$ or $(p \equiv q)$ where p and q are wffs of L;
3. Op where $O \in Mo$ and p is a wff of L;
4. $\forall xp$ or $\exists xp$ where p is a wff of L and x is an individual variable.

We think of L as a fragment of a second-order language $\mathscr{L}$. This is determined by the categories which determine L, i.e. Pr, X, and Mo. It differs from

L in allowing quantification over relations. We do not develop the syntax and semantics of $\mathscr{L}$ because references to $\mathscr{L}$ will be made only occasionally.

As regards the syntax of L, not many notions in addition to those in 1–4 will be required. If p and q are wffs of L, then p is called a component of q if and only if p is identical with q or with a well-formed part of q.

An occurrence of the individual variable x in p is bound in p if and only if a component of p of the kind $\forall xq$ or $\exists\, xq$ exhibits it. An occurrence of x in p is said to be free in p if and only if it is not bound in p.

If p is a wff that does not exhibit any free occurrence of variables, then it is said to be a sentence or a closed wff. A wff which is not a sentence is open.

If p is a wff, then $S_a^x p|$ shall denote the result of replacing each free occurrence of the individual variable x in p by the individual variable or constant a.

If $x_1, x_2, ..., x_n$ are the individual variables with free occurrences in p, $\forall x_1\, \forall x_2\, ... \forall x_n p$ is the universal closure of p. The universal closure of an open wff is of course a sentence.

A modal operator $O \in Mo$ may or may not be supplied with an index in the form of an individual variable or constant a; if it is, it will be referred to by O_a and said to denote a relative modality.

A convenient way to articulate the modality denoted by an operator $O \in Mo$, is to give the truth conditions of a wff of the kind Op. This method will be used in the sequel to characterize the modalities that are relevant for our purposes and basic to our approach. So we turn to the semantics of L.

2. ON THE SEMANTICS OF A FIRST-ORDER LANGUAGE

It is evident that a first-order language is obtained from L, if the category Mo and wffs containing symbols in Mo are removed. That is to say, $L(Pr, X, Mo)$ is a first-order language if Mo is empty. It is convenient to consider this case first in the construction of a model for L.

A model for $L(Pr, X)$ is a pair $M = (X, V)$, where V is a function which assigns to each k-place predicate letter $P \in Pr$ a k-place relation $V(P)$ on X, i.e. $V(P^k) \subseteq X^k$. (For the overall character of the semantics of L we are indebted to Robbin (1969, Chapter 2). Note in particular that no distinction is made between the class of constants in the language and the class of individuals denoted by constants.) The standard inductive definition of the relation that obtains between a sentence p of $L(Pr, X)$ when p holds or does not hold in M – expressed as $M \models p$ and $M \not\models p$, respectively – runs as follows:

(M.Pr) $M \models P(a_1, a_2, ..., a_k)$ if and only if $(a_1, a_2, ..., a_k) \in V(P)$;
(M.$\sim$) $M \models {\sim}p$ if and only if $M \not\models p$;

(M.&) $M \models (p \& q)$ if and only if $M \models p$ and $M \models q$;
(M.v) $M \not\models (p \vee q)$ if and only if $M \not\models p$ and $M \not\models q$;
(M.⊃) $M \not\models (p \supset q)$ if and only if $M \models p$ and $M \not\models q$;
(M.≡) $M \models (p \equiv q)$ if and only if $M \models p$ and $M \models q$ or $M \not\models p$ and $M \not\models q$;
(M.∀) $M \models \forall xp$ if and only if $M \models S_a^x p|$ for every $a \in X$;
(M.∃) $M \models \exists xp$ if and only if $M \models S_a^x p|$ for some $a \in X$.

An open wff of $L(Pr, X)$ holds in a model M if and only if its universal closure holds in M.

3. THE SEMANTICS FOR L

A model for L is essentially a class of first-order models, structured in a certain way. More precisely, a model for L is defined as a triple $\mathscr{M} = (U, R, M)$. Here U, the domain of the model, is a non-empty set of general points of reference indexing the first-order models; it is convenient to call these indices possible worlds. R is a function which assigns to each $O \in Mo$ a binary 'accessibility' relation $R(O)$ on U; the further conditions that $R(O)$ satisfies vary from case to case in accordance with the nature of the modality concerned. M is a function which assigns to each $u \in U$ a model $M(u) = (X_u, V_u)$ with $X_u \subseteq X$.

We can now define inductively the relation that obtains between a point of reference u in (the domain of) a model $\mathscr{M}$ and any sentence p when p holds or does not hold in $\mathscr{M}$ at u. The basis of the definition is given by the clause

(OM.Pr) $\mathscr{M} \models_{\overline{u}} P(a_1, a_2, ..., a_k)$ if and only if $M(u) \models P(a_1, a_2, ..., a_k)$, in which case $(a_1, a_2, ..., a_k) \in X_u^k$, $V_u(P) \subseteq X_u^k$ and $(a_1, a_2, ..., a_k) \in V_u(P)$.

The inductive clauses for $\models_{\overline{u}}$, in respect of sentences exhibiting a connective or a quantifier, are the same as their counterparts for the relation $\models$. For example, in the case of universal quantification we have the clause

(OM.∀) $\mathscr{M} \models_{\overline{u}} \forall xp$ if and only if $\mathscr{M} \models_{\overline{u}} S_a^x p|$ for every $a \in X_u$.

The inductive clauses for $\models_{\overline{u}}$, in respect of modalized sentences, take one of the following forms:

(OM1) $\mathscr{M} \models_{\overline{u}} Op$ if and only if $\mathscr{M} \models_{\overline{v}} p$ for each v such that $(u, v) \in R(O)$ and, in case $O = O_a$, $a \in X_u$;

(OM2) $\mathscr{M} \models_{\overline{u}} Op$ if and only if $\mathscr{M} \models_{\overline{v}} {\sim} p$ for each v such that $(u, v) \in R(O)$ and, in case $O = O_a$, $a \in X_u$.

The dual of Op in (OM1) is subject to the condition

(OM3) $\mathcal{M}\,|\!\overline{\overline{u}}\,\sim O \sim p$ if and only if $\mathcal{M}\,|\!\overline{\overline{v}}\,p$ for some v such that (u, v)
           $\in R(O)$ and, in case $O = O_a$, $a \in X_u$.

The dual of Op in (OM2) is similarly subject to the condition

(OM4) $\mathcal{M}\,|\!\overline{\overline{u}}\,\sim O \sim p$ if and only if $\mathcal{M}\,|\!\overline{\overline{v}}\,\sim p$ for some v such that (u, v)
           $\in R(O)$ and, in case $O = O_a$, $a \in X_u$.

There is now ready access to a number of standard semantic notions. In particular, an open wff of L is said to hold in $\mathcal{M}$ at u if and only if its universal closure holds in $\mathcal{M}$ at u. With $|\!\overline{\overline{u}}$ now everywhere defined in the class of wffs, the standard notion of logical consequence is available: q is a logical consequence of $p_1, p_2, ..., p_n$ $(n \geqslant 0)$ if and only if there is no model $\mathcal{M}$ such that, for some u, $\mathcal{M}\,|\!\overline{\overline{u}}\,p_i$, for every i from 1 to n, and $\mathcal{M}\,|\!\!\!\not\overline{\overline{u}}\,q$.

By the logic of L we understand the class of consequence relationships $p_1, p_2, ..., p_n \models q$ that hold according to the semantics of L. Not much will be said about the logic of L in this work, i.e. about the class as such, but comments on select members of the class occur *passim*.

4. NECESSITY FOR SOMETHING THAT AN AGENT DOES

So far the category of the assignments $R(O)$ in a model for L has been specified in general terms only. In this and the succeeding section two of them will be described in some detail, namely the two that are central in the analysis of action.

L, we may assume, contains wffs of the kind $D_a p$, translated as 'it is necessary for something which a does that p'. In Pörn (1970, pp. 9–11), the semantics of wffs of this kind was articulated under the reading 'a brings it about that p'. Following Kanger (1972, p. 108 and p. 111), it will now be rearticulated with the present, improved reading in mind.

Assume that a state of affairs, for example that a window is open or that a door bell is activated, is a feature of a situation u. We wish to say that it is necessary for something that an agent does in u. Evidently, the meaning intended here cannot be explicated by reference to u alone. It is well known that notions of necessity cannot be exhausted by considering only what is the case; consideration must also be given to what might be the case, i.e. to certain hypothetical situations. In the case at hand we must consider all those hypothetical situations u' in which the agent does at least as much as he does in u. If v is such a situation, it may be said to be possible relative to what the agent does in u. We express this by writing $(u, v) \in R(D_a)$, where a is the (name of the) agent concerned.

It is now easy to articulate the notion of necessity under consideration. For if p is necessary for something that a does in u, then there cannot be a situation which is possible relative to what a does in u and which lacks the state of affairs that p. In other words, (OM1) in the case where $O = D_a$, is the truth condition of sentences of the kind $D_a p$. The precise import of this condition depends of course on the properties of the relation $R(D_a)$. A natural minimal assumption is that the relation is reflexive and transitive in U. We let this assumption constitute our condition (OM5). One further condition concerning $R(D_a)$ will be introduced in the next section.

5. COUNTERACTION CONDITIONALITY

The basis of a causal theory of action will be presented in this chapter. The term 'causal' is appropriate here in view of the fact that the principal construction employed, *viz.* 'a brings it about that p', pertains to agent causality. It is not certain that this construction can be analysed in terms of anything simpler or more fundamental than itself. But it can be elaborated by means of concepts that make it possible to set out the principles of our reasoning with it.

One such concept is the concept of that which is necessary for something that an agent does, for it is plain that if he brings about p, then p is necessary for something that he does. To maintain the converse, as was done in Pörn (1970, 1971), has its disadvantages. The ascription of causality to an agent normally suggests either that but for his action it would not be the case that p or that but for his action it might not be the case that p. These notions of counteraction conditionality are not present in the concept of that which is necessary for something that an agent does. As evidence of this one may cite the fact about L that if it is logically necessary and hence unavoidable that p, then p is also necessary for something that an agent does.

Because of our interest in the concept of bringing about, and in view of the above comments, we make available in L the means of expressing counteraction conditionality, in the form of wffs of the kind $D_a' p$, which are translated as 'but for a's action it would not be the case that p'. In their truth condition we consider all those situations in which a does not do any of the things he does in a given situation. That is, for the articulation of the truth of $D_a' p$ at u we require all hypothetical situations u' such that the opposite of everything that a does in u is the case in u'. (Compare the treatment of Dò in Kanger (1972, p. 121).) If v is such a situation, we write

$(u, v) \in R(D'_a)$ and, setting $O = D'_a$ in (OM2), the desired truth condition is obtained. We further define this condition by requiring the relation $R(D'_a)$ to be irreflexive and serial, a requirement which we shall call (OM6).

Because of the presence of two modalities in the notion of bringing about we need some conditions to connect $R(D_a)$ and $R(D'_a)$. We shall make use of only one such condition, *viz.* the following:

(OM7)   If $(u, v_1) \in R(D_a)$ and $(u, v_2) \in R(D_a)$ then $(v_1, w) \in R(D'_a)$ if
        and only if $(v_2, w) \in R(D'_a)$.

(OM7) is a condition of considerable strength. It requires that worlds which are alternatives to a given world under the relation $R(D_a)$ be treated as equals in contexts of counteraction conditionality. In spite of its strength the condition appears reasonable, however. It implies the condition

(OM7.1) If $(u, v) \in R(D_a)$ and $(v, w) \in R(D'_a)$ then $(u, w) \in R(D'_a)$,

which says that the relative product $R(D_a) / R(D'_a)$ is a subset of $R(D'_a)$. The counterpart of this condition in the logic of L is the wff $(D'_a p \supset D_a D'_a p)$. Since the converse is also in the logic of L because $R(D_a)$ is reflexive the wff

(1) $(D'_a p \equiv D_a D'_a p)$

is valid.

(OM7) also implies the condition

(OM7.2) If $(u, v) \in R(D_a)$ and $(u, w) \in R(D'_a)$ then $(v, w) \in R(D'_a)$.

Its counterpart in the logic of L is the wff $(\sim D'_a \sim p \supset D_a \sim D'_a \sim p)$. Since the converse also holds the wff

(2) $(\sim D'_a \sim p \equiv D_a \sim D'_a \sim p)$

is valid. Thus, both strong and weak counteraction conditionality, expressed by $D'_a p$ and $\sim D'_a \sim p$, respectively, are always a necessity for something that the agent does.

6. SOME DEFINED ACTION CONCEPTS

In terms of the two relative modalities now available to us others may be defined. We first introduce the following convenient rewrites of the duals of $D_a p$ and $D'_a p$ evaluated by means of (OM3) and (OM4), respectively:

(Df1) $C_a p = \sim D_a \sim p$
(Df2) $C'_a p = \sim D'_a \sim p$

The first says that it is compatible with everything which a does that p, the second that but for a's activity it might not be the case that p. In view of the fact that $D_a'p$ may be read as 'p is dependent on a's action' and $D_a' \sim p$ as 'p is independent of a's action', an alternative reading of $C_a'p$ is 'p is not independent of a's action'.

It has already been pointed out that the agent-causal construction 'a brings it about that p' implies 'p is necessary for something that a does' and also 'but for a's action it would not be that p' or 'but for a's action it might not be that p'. Of these counteraction conditional propositions the first implies but is not implied by the second, since

(3) $(D_a'p \supset C_a'p)$

but not its converse is in the logic of L. It might be thought that the difference between them could be used to distinguish between two complex modalities pertaining to agent causality, *viz*. a weak action modality defined by

(Df3) $E_a p = (D_a p \ \& \ C_a'p)$

and a strong action modality defined by

(Df4) $E_a^* p = (D_a p \ \& \ D_a'p)$.

Which of these should be adopted as the analysis of 'a brings it about (causes it to be the case that, effects that) p'?

It may be shown that

(4) $(D_a'(p \supset q) \equiv (D_a' \sim p \ \& \ D_a' q))$

is valid. In view of (3) and (Df2) it may therefore also be seen that

(5) $(D_a' (p \supset q) \supset \sim D_a' p)$

holds. It follows immediately from (5) and (Df4) that

(6) $(E_a^*(p \supset q) \supset \sim E_a^* p)$

holds. Hence, if (Df4) is accepted, the conjunction of 'a brings it about that if p then q' and 'a brings it about that p' will be self-inconsistent. But there are many actions which can be adequately described only by means of such (consistent) conjunctions. We therefore reject (Df4) and accept (Df3) as the analysis of the agent-causal construction 'a brings it about that p'. (The argument against the use of (Df4) is due to Mr. A. J. I. Jones. A definition equivalent to (Df4) may be found in Kanger (1972, p. 108). In Chellas

(1969, Chapter III, Section 4), there is a definition of 'a sees to it that p' which, like the one given in Pörn (1971), makes the construction equivalent to the present $D_a p$. A definition which makes it equivalent to $E_a p$ may be found in Needham (1971, p. 154). Essentially the same idea is suggested in Hilpinen (1973, Section VI), and it is explicit in Pörn (1974, p. 96).)

The modality D_a' is subject to the rule

R1′   If $q \mid= (p_1 \vee p_2 \vee ... \vee p_n)$ then $D_a' p_1, D_a' p_2, ..., D_a' p_n \mid= D_a' q$

where in case $n = 0$, $q \mid=$ is understood as a rewrite of $\mid= \sim q$. Since $\sim p \mid= \sim E_a p$, an application of the rule shows that $D_a' \sim E_a p \mid= D_a' \sim p$. The wff $(D_a' \sim E_a p \supset D_a' \sim p)$ is therefore valid. After abbreviating its contraposition as per (Df1) we obtain the result that

(7) $(C_a' p \supset C_a' E_a p)$

is a valid wff. In view of (OM5)

(8) $(D_a p \supset D_a D_a p)$

holds. (2), (7) and (8) combine to yield

(9) $((D_a p \ \& \ C_a' p) \supset (D_a D_a p \ \& \ D_a C_a' p \ \& \ C_a' E_a p))$

which is logically equivalent to

(10) $((D_a p \ \& \ C_a' p) \supset (D_a (D_a p \ \& \ C_a' p) \ \& \ C_a' E_a p))$

because D_a is distributive over conjunction. If we now apply (Df3) we obtain the valid wff

(11) $(E_a p \supset E_a E_a p)$.

Because $R(D_a)$ is reflexive, according to (OM5), the wff $(D_a p \supset p)$ is valid and hence also $(E_a p \supset p)$ in view of the presence of $D_a p$ in $E_a p$. It follows that the converse of (11) is valid and, hence, that

(12) $(E_a p \equiv E_a E_a p)$

is valid.

We have at our disposal two basic action modalities and their duals. In (Df3) and (Df4) two pairs of concepts drawn from this basic set of four are employed. Other such pairs are of interest for our purposes. The definiens of

(Df5) $N_a p = (D_a p \ \& \ D_a' \sim p)$

says that p is necessary for something that a does and, in this sense, a practical necessity for a. The definiens further says that p is (counterfactually) independent of what a does. So $N_a p$ is to the effect that p is such a practical necessity for a as is independent of his action or, more briefly, that it is unavoidable for a that p.

For the dual of $N_a p$ we shall use the following rewrite:

(Df6) $M_a p = \sim N_a \sim p$

$M_a p$ is logically equivalent to $(C_a p \vee C_a' \sim p)$. The use of M_a for the purposes of referring to an agent's ability and opportunity to act is not unproblematic. We shall nevertheless use the modality in this way and we therefore take $M_a p$, 'it is possible for a that p', to mean that a can perform or that it is possible for a to perform an action *whenever p* expresses an action with a as agent. (A different but related notion of ability to do will be discussed in Section 32.) M_a and N_a have a number of logical properties which are suitable for this interpretation. For example,

(13) $(E_a p \supset M_a E_a p)$

is in the logic of L and so is

(14) $(M_a E_a p \supset M_a p)$

(but not the converse). Accordingly,

(15) $(N_a p \supset \sim M_a E_a \sim p)$

is valid.

The modalities N_a and E_a are subject to the law

(16) $(N_a(p \equiv q) \supset (E_a p \equiv E_a q))$

which is, as we shall see, a convenient and important feature of the joint behaviour of the two modalities.

The modalities defined in (Df5) and (Df6) may be generalized in the way shown in the following definitions:

(Df7) $Np = \forall x N_x p$
(Df8) $Mp = \exists x M_x p$

The most obvious features of the generalization are captured by

(17) $(Np \supset N_a p)$

and

(18) $(M_a p \supset Mp)$.

The role of the modalities N and M will become apparent later in this chapter.

7. ON THE LOGIC OF L

Here we shall list some members of the logic of L, namely those that exhibit features of the central modalities already introduced together with the modality F_a which will be introduced in Section 10. To facilitate the presentation of these members and to make for ease of comparison, we first list the following rules and forms for a modal operator O, which may or may not express a relative modality:

R1   If $p_1, p_2, ..., p_n \models q$ then $Op_1, Op_2, ..., Op_n \models Oq$.

R2   If $\models (p \equiv q)$ then $\models (Op \equiv Oq)$.

F1 $\models (Op \supset p)$.

F2 $\models (Op \supset {\sim}O{\sim}p)$.

F3 $\models (O(p \supset q) \supset (Op \supset Oq))$.

F4 $\models (O(p \lor q) \supset (Op \lor Oq))$.

F5 $\models ((Op \lor Oq) \supset O(p \lor q))$.

F6 $\models (O(p \,\&\, q) \supset (Op \,\&\, Oq))$.

F7 $\models ((Op \,\&\, Oq) \supset O(p \,\&\, q))$.

F8 $\models (O\forall xp \supset \forall xOp)$.

F9 $\models (\forall xOp \supset O\forall xp)$.

F10 $\models (O\exists xp \supset \exists xOp)$.

F11 $\models (\exists xOp \supset O\exists xp)$.

The consequence relationships indicated by $+$ in the array in the following table belong, and those indicated by $-$ do not belong, to the logic of L.

TABLE I

Some logical characteristics of basic modalities

0	R1	R2	F1	F2	F3	F4	F5	F6	F7	F8	F9	F10	F11
D_a	+ for $n \geqslant 0$	+	+	+	+	−	+	+	+	+	−	−	+
C_a	+ for $n = 0,1$	+	−	−	−	+	+	+	−	+	−	−	+
D_a'	−	+	−	+	+	+	−	−	+	−	+	+	−
C_a'	−	+	−	−	+	+	−	−	+	−	+	+	−
E_a	−	+	+	+	+	−	−	−	+	−	−	−	−
F_a	−	+	+	+	+	−	−	−	+	−	+	+	−
N_a	+ for $n \geqslant 0$	+	+	+	+	−	+	+	+	+	−	−	+
M_a	+ for $n = 0,1$	+	−	−	−	+	+	+	−	+	−	−	+

We note in particular that R1 does not hold for E_a. In this respect there is an important difference between E_a and D_a, which gives the former a definite advantage as a tool in the analysis of action concepts. Instead of R1 for D_a' we have the rule R1$'$, formulated in Section 6. We also note that E_a^* is like

E_a, N like N_a, and M like M_a, with respect to the logical characteristics featured in Table I.

8. ACT RELATIONS

In Section 5 we hinted at a causal theory of action. We shall now formulate this theory. The problem it is intended to solve is easily introduced. There is an intuitive difference between, for example, the property of giving a lecture and the property of growing old. Anyone who exemplifies the former acts in a certain way. This is not true of the latter. So giving a lecture is an act property, growing old is not. Similarly, there is an intuitive difference between the dyadic relations of kicking and being taller than. The first is, the second is not, an act relation. If we admit the jargon according to which properties are relations, namely one-place relations, we may say, quite generally, that there is a distinction to be made between act relations and all other relations. How should this distinction be made? This is the characterization problem for act relations.

The intuitively most obvious difference between the relations of kicking and being taller than is the circumstance that if a pair (a, b) satisfies both relations, this is a fact which is brought about by the agent a in the case of the first relation whereas in the case of the second relation it is independent of what a and b do. If p is an n-place relation ($n \geqslant 1$), we shall therefore say that p is an act relation only if

$$(19) \qquad \forall x_1 \forall x_2 \ldots \forall x_n (p \supset E_{x_i} p)$$

is true for some i from 1 to n. Since F1 holds for E_{x_i}, we may also say that p is an n-place act relation only if

$$(20) \qquad \forall x_1 \forall x_2 \ldots \forall x_n (p \equiv E_{x_i} p)$$

is true for some i from 1 to n. This is clearly not also a sufficient condition, for it is the case that

$$(21) \qquad \forall x (\sim(x = x) \equiv E_x \sim(x = x))$$

but we would not therefore say that the relation of not being self-identical is an act relation. To make the criterion adequate we must further require that the predicate $E_{x_i} p$ in (20) can apply to or be true of some agent. We incorporate this requirement in the following definition, which is our solution to the characterization problem for act relations. (Compare Kanger (1972, p. 123), on the characterization problem for acting, and Pörn (1974), on the definition of an act predicate.)

(Df9)   If p is an n-place relation ($n \geqslant 1$), then it is an n-place act relation if and only if

$$(\forall x_1 \forall x_2 \ldots \forall x_n \, (p \equiv E_{x_i} p) \ \& \ M \, \exists x_1 \, \exists x_2 \ldots \exists x_n \, E_{x_i} p)$$

is true for some i from 1 to n.

To illustrate, let us consider the following propositions:

(22) $\forall x ((x \text{ is growing old}) \equiv E_x (x \text{ is growing old}))$;
(23) $M \exists x E_x (x \text{ is growing old})$;
(24) $\forall x \forall y ((x \text{ kisses } y) \equiv E_x (x \text{ kisses } y))$;
(25) $M \exists x \exists y E_x (x \text{ kisses } y)$;
(26) $\forall x \forall y ((x \text{ kisses } y) \equiv E_y (x \text{ kisses } y))$;
(27) $M \exists x \exists y E_y (x \text{ kisses } y)$.

In view of (Df9), growing old is an act property if and only if (22) and (23) are both true. Similarly, the relation of kissing is a dyadic act relation if and only if (24) and (25) are both true or else (26) and (27) are both true.

We note that if p is an act relation, then the relation expressed by the predicate $E_{x_i} p$ is also an act relation. This may be seen to be so because, for each i from 1 to n,

(28) $\forall x_1 \forall x_2 \ldots \forall x_n (E_{x_i} p \equiv E_{x_i} E_{x_i} p)$

is a logical truth in view of (12). It follows that

(29) $(\exists x_1 \exists x_2 \ldots \exists x_n E_{x_i} p \equiv \exists x_1 \exists x_2 \ldots \exists x_n E_{x_i} E_{x_i} p)$

is a logical truth for each i from 1 to n and, hence, because of the validity of R2 for M, that

(30) $(M \exists x_1 \exists x_2 \ldots \exists x_n E_{x_i} p \equiv M \exists x_1 \exists x_2 \ldots \exists x_n E_{x_i} E_{x_i} p)$

is a logical truth. So if p is an act relation, the right-hand side of (30) is true, in which case its conjunction with (29) is also true, i.e. the relation expressed by the predicate $E_{x_i} p$ is an act relation. More generally, if we let $E_{x_i}^1 = E_{x_i}$ and $E_{x_i}^{n+1} = E_{x_i} E_{x_i}^n$, it may be shown that if p is an act relation, so is the relation expressed by $E_{x_i}^n p$ (for $n \geqslant 1$ and for each i from 1 to n). The latter relations are obviously all equal, i.e. they have exactly the same members, and they are equal to p whenever p is an act relation.

The n-tuples that satisfy an act relation (at a given time) may be termed its instances (at that time). We shall often use "action" as a compendious term covering both act relations and their instances. If p is an act relation and the n-tuple $(a_1, a_2, ..., a_n)$ satisfies this relation, then, pursuant to (Df9), we shall say that a_i $(i = 1, 2, ..., n)$ is the agent of the action (act instance) concerned if and only if a_i brings it about that $p(a_1, a_2, ..., a_n)$.

The objection might be raised that our characterization of an action is circular. For in order for a state of affairs p to be an action with a as agent, $E_a p$ must be true. The agent-causal modality E_a which is used essentially here is defined in (Df3) by means of D_a and C'_a. But these, according to the reasoning outlined in Sections 4 and 5, are in turn partly characterized in terms of what a does: $D_a p$ means that p is necessary for something that a does and $C'_a p$ that but for a's action p might not be the case. Thus in our specification of a state of affairs as an action with a as agent we rely on references to what a does, and it is this move which constitutes the circle.

It cannot be denied that our characterization is circular in the sense just described. But the circle does not appear to be vicious. On the contrary, our way of specifying states of affairs as actions is extremely useful because it relies on terms that allow us to exhibit the principles of our reasoning concerning agency. Our analysis supplies a method for selecting, in the case of any given construction, that part of it, if any, which refers to an agent or active source, and for doing this in a systematic fashion. One example, which, as we shall see later, is crucial for the understanding of the so-called Ross's Paradox, will illustrate this point. In virtue of the fact that R1 does not hold for E_a, it is not the case that $E_a p \models E_a (p \vee q)$, though, of course, $p \models (p \vee q)$. It follows that the assumption that $E_a p$ expresses an action does *not* imply that $E_a (p \vee q)$ also expresses an action. And this, in turn, has obvious consequences for the use of R1 as applied to deontic or normative modalities. (That a definition such as (Df9) must be circular in the way indicated, is powerfully argued in Taylor (1966, esp. Chapters 5–9).)

9. ACT RELATIONS AND N-EQUALITY

It is true that

(31) $((b \text{ kills } c) \equiv E_b (c \text{ is dead}))$.

It is also true that

(32) $(E_a (b \text{ kills } c) \equiv E_a E_b (c \text{ is dead}))$

but (31) does not logically imply (32). If the implication is to hold in our logic, the equivalence in (31) must be strengthened somehow. Because R2 holds for E_a the implication would of course be valid if we took (31) to be logically true. This we cannot do, however, for (31) is not logically true, only analytically true. In other cases where an implication of the kind under consideration holds the equivalence involved may not be analytically true but, say, an extra-linguistic truth, e.g. an instance of a regular connection in nature.

The most suitable species of necessity to rely on here seems to be that of unavoidability. If this is correct, (31) should be replaced by

$$(33) \qquad N_a((b \text{ kills } c) \equiv E_b (c \text{ is dead})),$$

in which case the implication under consideration may be taken to be of form (16).

(16) suggests a principle for act relations. In order to state this we first introduce an auxiliary notion, that of N-equality between relations:

(Df10)   Let p and q be two n-place relations $(n \geqslant 1)$. Then p and q are N-equal if and only if

$$N \, \forall x_1 \, \forall x_2 \, ... \, \forall x_n (p \equiv q)$$

is true.

Using (16) and (17) in union with (Df9) and (Df10) the following principle may now readily be proved: if p and q are N-equal relations, then p is an act relation if and only if q is an act relation.

The suggestion might be made that the notion of N-equality is more closely connected with the notion of an act relation that it appears from the principle just stated − that the former notion should be used in the explication of the latter in the following way:

(Df11)   If p is an n-place relation $(n \geqslant 1)$, then it is an n-place act relation if and only if

$$(N \, \forall x_1 \, \forall x_2 \, ... \, \forall x_n (p \equiv E_{x_i} p) \, \& \, M \exists \, x_1 \, \exists x_2 \, ... \, \exists x_n p)$$

is true for some i from 1 to n.

Should (Df11) rather than (Df9) be adopted? An important difference between them is due to the fact that

$$(34) \qquad (N_a p \supset {\sim} E_a p)$$

is in the logic of L. For it follows, in view of (17), that if (Df11) is accepted, then nobody can bring about the equivalence that is characteristic of act relations. It follows, for example, that

(35) $E_a \forall x ((a \text{ greets } x) \equiv E_x (a \text{ greets } x))$

must be false, if the property that x has just in case a greets x is an act property in the sense of (Df11). But (35) might be true along with $M \exists x$ (a greets x) and is it then not acceptable to say, despite the truth of (35), that the property concerned is an act property? We wish to leave open the possibility of an affirmative answer to this question and we have therefore adopted (Df9), but we admit that the choice between the two definitions is problematic.

(35) is logically equivalent to

(36) $E_a (\forall x ((a \text{ greets } x) \supset E_x (a \text{ greets } x)) \ \& \ \forall x (E_x (a \text{ greets } x) \supset (a \text{ greets } x)))$.

It must not be thought that (36) and therefore (35) are false because the second conjunct in (36) is unavoidably true (because it is logically true) and hence, in view of (34), cannot be made true through agency. E_a is not distributive over conjunction. $E_a (p \ \& \ q)$ is compatible with the unavoidable truth of one of the conjuncts, for

(37) $(N_a p \supset ((p \ \& \ E_a q) \equiv E_a (p \ \& \ q)))$

is in the logic of L. (36) and its equivalent (35) are therefore true as soon as

(38) $E_a \forall x ((a \text{ greets } x) \supset E_x (a \text{ greets } x))$

is true.

It may be of some interest to note that (Df11) can be generalized in the following way:

(Df12)   If p is an n-place relation ($n \geqslant 1$), then it is an n-place act relation if an only if there is a relation or state of affairs q such that

$(N \forall x_1 \forall x_2 \ ... \ \forall x_n (p \equiv E_{x_i} q) \ \& \ M \exists \ x_1 \ \exists \ x_2 \ ... \ \exists x_n p)$

is true for some i from 1 to n.

To illustrate, let q be the state of affairs that a designated individual a is dead. According to (Df12) the property of killing a is then an act property if and only if, first, it is unavoidably the case that, for any x, x kills a if and only if x brings it about that a is dead and, secondly, it is possible that there be somebody who kills a.

To prove that a relation which is an act relation as per (Df11) is also an act relation as per (Df12), we only need to let q be p itself. The proof of the converse is not forthcoming because

(39) $(N_a p \supset N_a N_a p)$

is not a logical truth. (Df12) is therefore a genuine extension of (Df11). ((39) would be valid if $R(D'_a)$ was a transitive relation, in which case $(D'_a p \supset D'_a \sim D'_a p)$ would be valid.) This means that (Df11) and (Df12) are equivalent in the class of relations p for which (39) is true.

10. CONSEQUENCES OF ACTION

Suppose that an agent a starts a fire in his garden. At the time the circumstances are as good as any as far as fire control is concerned, but later the wind freshens, the fire gets out of control, sweeps towards a neighbour's house and destroys it. Destroying the house by fire is clearly not necessary for something which a does, for it is possible for there to be a situation which is $R(D_a)$-related to the situation described and in which a does not destroy the neighbour's house by fire. In some situations which are $R(D_a)$-relatives of the given situation the fire destroys a's own house, in some others it destroys no houses at all, and so on. Destroying the house by fire therefore has a different status from setting the fire going; the latter is the case in any situation which is an $R(D_a)$-relative of the given situation. For this reason it would not be true to say that a destroys the neighbour's house by fire.

Although the destruction of the house is not an action with a as agent, it is related to a's agency, if it is true, and this is highly probable, that the house might not have been destroyed, as and when it actually was destroyed, but for a's action of setting the fire going. We shall capture this relation to a's agency by saying that the destruction of the house is a consequence of something which a does and, as already indicated, we shall make weak counterfactual dependence an ingredient of this concept of a consequence of action. We define the modality involved thus:

(Df13) $F_a p = (p \ \& \ C'_a p)$

$F_a p$ may be read as 'it follows from something a does that p' or 'p is a consequence of something a does'. A narrower notion of an action consequence may be obtained within our framework by replacing C'_a in (Df13) by D'_a. The narrower notion is relevant when agency is regarded with a view to the ascription of responsibility.

Some logical features of F_a were specified in Section 7. A further feature is that the counterpart of (16) holds for F_a. But, more interestingly, a weakened version of (16) is forthcoming, for a notion that is weaker than N_a may be defined thus:

(Df14) $I_a p = (p \mathbin{\&} D'_a \sim p)$

Here the definiens says that p is the case independently of what a does. Necessity of this kind, often in the generalized form $\forall x I_x p$, seems to be prominent when we speak of natural necessities. It is subject to the law

(40) $(I_a (p \equiv q) \supset (F_a p \equiv F_a q))$

and it is like the modality N_a with respect to the logical characteristics featured in the table in Section 7.

In this book we rely on the notion of bringing about rather than that of an action consequence, but we shall have reason to make some use of the latter, primarily in Chapter 5.

CHAPTER 2

INTENTIONS AND REASONS

So far no mention has been made of intention in the context of actions. Our solution to the characterization problem for action is compatible with different ways of defining intentional action and other concepts of intention. In view of this fact and the consideration that a comprehensive theory of action should cover intentional action and related matters we suggest in this chapter solutions to the following characterization problems: What is an intention to perform an action? What is an intentional action? What is the nature of an action done with a further intention? To refer to these concepts of intention we shall use the following constructions, respectively: (i) 'a intends to bring it about that p', (ii) 'a brings it about that p intentionally', and (iii) 'a brings it about that p with the intention of bringing it about that q' or, equivalently, 'a brings it about that p in order to bring it about that q'. The use of these as prototype constructions is natural and immediate from the point of view of our analysis of action in the previous chapter. We conclude the present chapter by contrasting the concepts of intention with certain notions pertaining to reasons for action. The concept of belief and a number of normative notions are prominent in our account of the three concepts of intention. They will therefore be introduced first.

11. BELIEF

Constructions of the form $B_a p$ in L are read as 'a believes that p', 'a is of the opinion that p', 'a is convinced that p', 'a is certain that p', etc. These readings may all be grouped together because the differences of nuance between them are immaterial for our purposes.

How should $B_a p$ be understood semantically? Let us remind ourselves that the intuitive meaning of 'a believes that p' is 'a accepts p as true'. We shall understand this to imply that the truth value of $B_a p$ is determined by the truth value, if any, that p has at certain points in a model. However, the elements of U, as we have understood them so far, force the truth or falsity of any wff. In other words, they do not admit truth value gaps. But it seems plain that it is necessary to admit such gaps, if we are to capture the sort of selective attention that is an obvious feature of belief. So we shall introduce elements into U which do not necessarily force the truth or falsity of just any wff, and to mark the difference between these and normal elements or possible worlds, we shall distinguish between the relations $|\!\!\overline{\overline{u}}$ and $\|\!\!\overline{\overline{u}}$.

The definition of $|\!\!\overline{\overline{u}}$ has been given in general terms. To define $\|\!\!\overline{\overline{u}}$ we need to extend a model for L by adding a function M'. So by a model for L we are now to understand a structure $\mathcal{M} = (U, R, M, M')$, where U, R, and M are as before and M' is a function such that for $u \in U, M'(u) = (X'_u, V'_u)$. Here X'_u is the class of objects which are believed to be referents at U or, equivalently, the class of constants taken to have denotation at u. Obviously, X'_u need not coincide with X_u: it is possible for existing things not to be referred to and it is possible to refer to things that do not exist. V'_u determines the extension of predicates in Pr of $L(Pr, X, Mo)$ and, unlike V_u, it may be a partial function, i.e. it need not fix an extension for just any predicate in X'_u for an arbitrary u.

We may now define the relation $\|\!\!\overline{\overline{u}}$ and we begin with the following basic cases: ·

(M'.Pr) $\mathcal{M} \|\!\!\overline{\overline{u}} P(a_1, a_2, ..., a_k)$ if and only if $M'(u) \|\!= P(a_1, a_2, ..., a_k)$, in which case $(a_1, a_2, ..., a_k) \in X'^k_u$, $V'_u(P^k) \subseteq X'^k_u$, and $(a_1, a_2, ..., a_k) \in V'_u(P^k)$.

(M'.~Pr) $\mathcal{M} \|\!\!\overline{\overline{u}} \sim P(a_1, a_2, ..., a_k)$ if and only if $M'(u) \|\!= \sim P(a_1, a_2, ..., a_k)$, in which case $(a_1, a_2, ..., a_k) \in X'^k_u$, $V'_u(P^k) \subseteq X'^k_u$, and $(a_1, a_2, ..., a_k) \notin V'_u(P^k)$.

In the former case the atomic sentence $P(a_1, a_2, ..., a_k)$ is true at u, in the latter case it is false at u. So, according to (M'.Pr) and (M'.~Pr), an atomic sentence is false at a point if and only if its negation is true at that point. Further, if the sentence is true, it follows that it is not false. But if it is not true (false), it does not follow that it is false (true). This is one of the differences between $|\!\!\overline{\overline{u}}$ and $\|\!\!\overline{\overline{u}}$. For $\|\!\!\overline{\overline{u}}$

(i) $\|\!\!\overline{\overline{u}} p$
(ii) $\|\!\!\overline{\overline{u}} \sim p$
(iii) $\|\!\!\!\!/\!\overline{\overline{u}} p$ and $\|\!\!\!\!/\!\overline{\overline{u}} \sim p$

are all genuine possibilities; in the case of $|\!\!\overline{\overline{u}}$, however, (iii) vanishes. For the purposes of the definition of $\|\!\!\overline{\overline{u}}$, we say that the atomic sentence p has a truth value at u, if either case (i) or case (ii) obtains, and we say that it lacks a truth value, if case (iii) obtains.

The inductive clauses of the definition of $\|\!\!\overline{\overline{u}}$, in respect of sentential connectives, are governed by the following two principles:

(Comp. 1) A molecular sentence has a truth value at u in $\mathscr{M}$ if and only if all of its components have a truth value at u in $\mathscr{M}$.

(Comp. 2) If a molecular sentence has a truth value at u in $\mathscr{M}$, then this is determined by the truth value of its components in the usual way.

These principles immediately give us the conditions (OM$'$.&), (OM$'$.~&), (OM$'$.~v), etc.

Quantifications are dealt with in a parallel fashion. We illustrate by considering universal quantifications. We have:

(Comp. 3) A sentence of the form $\forall xp$ has a truth value at u if and only if $S_a^x p\,|$, for every $a \in X_u'$, has a truth value at u.

(OM$'$.$\forall$) $\mathscr{M} \parallel_{\overline{u}} \forall xp$ if and only if $\parallel_{\overline{u}} S_a^x p\,|$ for every $a \in X_u'$.

(OM$'$.~$\forall$) $\mathscr{M} \parallel_{\overline{u}} {\sim}\forall xp$ if and only if $\parallel_{\overline{u}} {\sim}S_a^x p\,|$ for some $a \in X_u'$.

Modalized sentences are entirely analogous. Hence:

(Comp. 4) A sentence of the form Op has a truth value at u if and only if p has a truth value at every point v such that $(u, v) \in R(O)$.

(OM$'$1) (a) $\mathscr{M} \parallel_{\overline{u}} Op$ if and only if $\mathscr{M} \parallel_{\overline{v}} p$ for every v such that $(u, v) \in R(O)$ and, in case $O = O_a$, $a \in X_u'$;

(b) $\mathscr{M} \parallel_{\overline{u}} {\sim}Op$ if and only if $\mathscr{M} \parallel_{\overline{v}} {\sim}p$ for some v such that $(u, v) \in R(O)$ and, in case $O = O_a$, $a \in X_u'$.

(OM1)–(OM4) could be said to define normal (positive or negative) modalities; truth values in *total* models exhaust the meaning of a normal modality. Belief-modalities, by contrast, are non-normal in their dependence on truth values in partial models. For B_a we suggest the following condition:

(OM.B_a) $\mathscr{M} \mid_{\overline{u}} B_a p$ if and only if $\mathscr{M} \parallel_{\overline{v}} p$ for every v such that $(u, v) \in R(B_a)$ and $a \in X_u$.

Here $(u, v) \in R(B_a)$ means that everything which a believes in u is the case in v. $R(B_a)$ cannot be assumed to be reflexive in U, for on this assumption, belief, like knowledge, would entail truth, and it clearly does not. But belief is thought governed by the ideal of attaining truth. Accordingly we treat $R(B_a)$ as an idealization relation and assume, minimally, that it is serial (for those individuals who are to count as believers). When $R(B_a)$ is understood in this way (OM.B_a) validates F2, F3, F6, F7, and F11. That we accept F2 does of course not mean that we rule out inconsistent belief as a logical impossibility. There really is no need to articulate inconsistent beliefs in terms of believing that $(p \ \& \sim p)$. The statement that a's belief that p is (self-) inconsistent can naturally be understood to mean that $B_a p$ and, in addition, that $p \models (q \ \& \sim q)$.

The very general rules R1 and R2 do not hold for B_a. Instead we have two more specialized rules. Let us call the signs that determine L the *descriptive* signs of L. The classes Pr, X and Mo exhaust the descriptive signs of L. Let us also say that $p_1, p_2, ..., p_n (n \geqslant 1)$ *cover* q if the descriptive signs of q are among the descriptive signs of $p_1, p_2, ..., p_n$. We may use this terminology to state two rules that hold for B_a. They are:

R3   If $p_1, p_2, ..., p_n \models q$ then $B_a p_1, B_a p_2, ..., B_a p_n \models B_a q$ provided that $p_1, p_2, ..., p_n$ cover q.

R4   If $\models (p \equiv q)$ then $\models (B_a p \equiv B_a q)$ provided that p covers q and q covers p.

So we have, for example, the results

$$\models (B_a E_b p \supset B_a p)$$
$$\models (B_a (p \supset p) \equiv B_a (\sim p \vee p))$$

but we do not have results like

$$\models (B_a p \supset B_a (p \vee q))$$
$$\models (B_a p \equiv B_a (p \ \& (q \vee \sim q)))$$

12. NORMS AND NORMATIVE POSITIONS

We next turn to the normative notions that are prominent in our account of the three concepts of intention. Intuitively, a norm assigns tasks to agents. Thus a norm is not a statistical regularity, as when we say that the weather is 'normal' for the season. A norm states what an agent should or should not do, or may or may not do, under specified circumstances. For example, the instructions for replacing tap washers or treating lavatory blockings, found in any comprehensive book of home management, are norms. So are the rules, laws, or statutes, or the regulations governing a society, class or profession. The following is a formulation of a norm: 'An alien who is resident in the U.K. and who changes his normal place of residence from the one last recorded in his Certificate of Registration shall report the change to the Police within 7 days of his arrival at the new address.' We may put this into the form

(1) $\forall x (r(x) \supset (p(x) \supset \text{Shall } q(x)))$

where $r(x)$ is short for 'x is an alien', $p(x)$ is short for 'x is resident in the U.K. and changes his normal place of residence from the one last recorded in his Certificate of Registration', and $q(x)$ is short for 'x reports the change to the Police within 7 days of his arrival at the new address'. In this formulation $r(x)$ states the *restriction*, $p(x)$ the *condition*, and $q(x)$ the *prescription* of the norm. (This convenient terminology is taken from Stenius (1972, p. 142).) The restriction defines the class of norm subjects, the prescription specifies a task, i.e. an action which a norm subject is to do if the norm condition is fulfilled. The employment of Shall in the task-specification of (1) is natural because this is one of the modalities that we use to refer to the result or outcome of action of type decision.

(1) is the characteristic form of a common type of norm formulation. A more general form is

(2) $\forall x (r(x) \supset Q_i Q_2 ... Q_m (p \supset Q_i Q_2 ... Q_n \, Tq(x)))$

where Q_i, $1 \leqslant i \leqslant m$, n, is a (possibly redundant) quantifier and $Tq(x)$ expresses a normative (legal) position.

For the purposes of explicating intentions to do only singular norms are relevant. Such a norm assigns a task to a designated subject on a condition. A singular norm, with the agent a as the designated norm subject, is expressed by a sentence of the form

(3) $Q_1 Q_2 ... Q_m (p \supset Q_1 Q_2 ... Q_n \, Tq(a))$.

Moreover, for the same purposes the role of the quantifiers is not of any decisive importance. We shall therefore simplify matters by taking the formulation of a singular norm to be of the form

(4) $(p \supset Tq(a))$.

Normative positions are defined in terms of the modality Shall ('It shall be the case that') and standard logical means. A wff of the kind Shall p is evaluated with the help of (OM1). That $(u, v) \in R$ (Shall) means that everything that is prescribed (decided) in u is the case in v or, for short, that v is a normative ideal of u. If we assume, as is quite customary in normative logic, that R(Shall) is a serial relation in U, i.e. that every member of U has at least one normative ideal, then R1, R2, F2, F3, F5–F8, and F11 hold for Shall. For the dual of Shall we introduce the abbreviation

(Df15)   May $p = \sim$Shall$\sim p$.

In order to further elucidate the concept of a norm we shall here briefly state the rudiments of the theory of normative (legal) positions. (For the most advanced study of this theory, see Lindahl (1977, Chapters 1–5). For its first formulation, see Kanger and Kanger (1966). See also Pörn (1970, Chapters 2–4), where the theory is stated together with the parallel theory for influence.) Normative positions may be defined for $n (n \geqslant 1)$ agents, and they may be simple or complex. The starting point of the theory of simple one-agent positions is set by the observation that the disjunction of

$$(5) \quad \begin{array}{ll} \text{(i)} & E_a p \\ \text{(ii)} & E_a \sim p \\ \text{(iii)} & \sim(E_a p \vee E_a \sim p) \end{array}$$

is complete and exhaustive, i.e. exactly one of (i)–(iii) is true for any a and any p. Each of these cases may be prescribed, proscribed, or neither prescribed nor proscribed. We can list the ways in which they can be consistently prescribed, proscribed or neither prescribed nor proscribed together. There are seven such ways. If we let + indicate that a case holds and − that it does not hold, we can list the ways as in the array of the following wffs.

(6.	1	2	3	4	5	6	7)
Shall $E_a p$	+	−	−	−	−	−	−
Shall $\sim E_a p$	−	+	+	+	−	−	−
Shall $E_a \sim p$	−	+	−	−	−	−	−
Shall $\sim E_a \sim p$	+	−	+	−	+	−	−
Shall $\sim(E_a p \vee E_a \sim p)$	−	−	+	−	−	−	−
Shall $(E_a p \vee E_a \sim p)$	+	+	−	−	−	+	−

(For some comments on (5), see Section 31. A list equivalent to (6) may be obtained by proving that May (5) is a truth of logic and logically equivalent to

$$(6') \qquad (\text{May (i)} \vee \text{May (ii)} \vee \text{May (iii)}))$$

which must therefore also be a truth of logic. The list comprising the seven possible truth cases of $(6')$ is equivalent to (6). This is the method used in Lindahl (1977).) The ways listed may be used to define the basic types of simple normative positions. More precisely, since the initial disjunction (5) is defined for one agent and (1)–(7) of (6) accordingly make an explicit reference to just one agent, the conjunctions may be used to define the seven basic types of simple one-agent normative positions. These can be thought of as sets of ordered pairs. For example, the set of all ordered pairs (a, p) such that

(6.1)   (Shall $E_a p$ & May $E_a p$ & May $\sim E_a \sim p$ & Shall $\sim E_a \sim p$ &
              May $(E_a p \vee E_a \sim p)$ & Shall $(E_a p \vee E_a \sim p)$)

is true constitutes type 1 of simple one-agent normative positions. A quick calculation will establish that a pair (a, p) is of type 1 if and only if Shall $E_a p$.

The theory may be extended to cover the basic types of simple two-agent positions and, more generally, n-agent positions. (For this theory and its specification as a theory of right relations, see Lindahl (1977, Chapters 1 and 4). For the theory of two-agent right relations, see also Kanger and Kanger (1966), and Pörn (1970, Chapter 4).) By applying set operations to types and, ultimately, to basic types it is possible to define non-basic types of simple n-agent positions. The theory for complex normative positions proceeds from the joint assertion of two or more disjunctions of type (5). For example, if we assert (5) for two distinct states of affairs and one agent, we obtain a complete and exhaustive disjunction of 9 terms, which can be made the point of departure of the theory of complex one-agent normative positions. This theory may in turn be extended to cover complex n-agent positions. To take just one illustration, Shall$(E_a p \vee E_a q)$ expresses a complex one-agent position whereas Shall$(E_a p \vee E_b q)$ expresses a complex two-agent position.

13. SINGULAR NORMS AND INTENTIONS TO DO

It seems natural to distinguish between the following two questions: (i) the question of the nature of an intention, and (ii) the question: under what circumstances will or is the agent likely to do that which he intends to do? Some writers believe that it is possible to give a general answer to question (ii), and this answer is often thought of as an answer also to question (i). There is, in other words, a tendency to collapse the two questions into one and to say that the nature of an intention can be exhausted by a suitably qualified prediction or by a suitably qualified statement of a disposition to act. (For a clear and detailed approach of this type, see Nordenfelt (1974).) We take the view that this tendency should be resisted. We therefore prefer to maintain the distinction between (i) and (ii). Here we will deal with the first question; and in the following section one aspect of the problem concerning the relation between intention and action will be taken up.

Central to the concept of intention, as exercised in constructions of the form

(7) a intends to bring it about that q if p,

is the notion of something to be done by a if p is the case. It is therefore natural to think that the norm expressed by

(8) $(p \supset \text{Shall } E_a q)$

is a's intention in this case. If so, how should (7) be articulated, or the idea that a has the intention in question? We think that a reference to a's belief is essential here. More precisely, we think that the singular norm expressed by (8) is a's intention to bring q about on the condition that p if and only if it occurs in the context of the belief expressed by

(9) $B_a (p \supset \text{Shall } E_a q)$

So (9) is our explication of (7). According to this conception, to intend is to hold a belief the content of which is a singular norm concerning one's own action. (9) may be compared with

(10) $B_b (p \supset \text{Shall } E_a q)$

which expresses that b *expects* a to bring about q if p. So (8) may express a's intention or b's expectation vis-à-vis a. In either case the singular norm has 'notional' existence, i.e. exists as the content of a belief held by a believer. (A normative expectation of type (10) should not be confused with a factual expectation of the kind $B_b (p \supset E_a q)$; the first belief, but not the second, is compatible with the statement that b does not think that a will bring q about if p obtains.)

The formation of a belief of type (9) may be termed a *decision* whenever (9) expresses an action. In this case (9) is equivalent to

(11) $E_a B_a (p \supset \text{Shall } E_a q)$

which represents our analysis of 'a decides to bring q about if p'. (11) may be compared with

(12) $E_b B_b (p \supset \text{Shall } E_a q)$

which says that b decides that a shall bring q about if p.

14. SETS AND SYSTEMS OF NORMS

That an agent intends to do something on a condition should not be confused with his belief that a norm is valid in a set of norms or with his belief that a norm exists or is in force. This is a point of some importance for the appreciation of our explication of (7). We shall therefore say something about sets and systems of norms and some cognate notions.

Let K be a class of norms. Suppose K contains the norm expressed by

(13)   All citizens who have attained the age of 18 may vote in general elections.

Since a citizen who is 20 years of age has attained the age of 18, (13) clearly implies

(14)   All citizens who are 20 years of age may vote in general elections.

But this fact does not warrant the conclusion that K also contains the norm expressed by (14), for we may suppose that there is in K exactly one norm, namely the one expressed by (13), concerning the right to vote in general elections.

However, though set K of norms containing (13) need not also contain (14), it is on the other hand plain that the latter is 'valid', in some sense, in any set K that contains the former. How should this notion of validity be understood? The above example gives us a clue here.

Whenever a class K of norms is given, e.g. by means of a list, we may define a class S_K of norms by the following procedure:

1. $K \subseteq S_K$
2. If there is a sequence $p_1, p_2, ..., p_n$ $(n \geqslant 0)$ of formulations of norms in S_K and, for some norm formulation q, $p_1, p_2, ..., p_n \models q$, possibly in virtue of a set of presupposed logical, analytical or mathematical truths, then the norm expressed by q is also a member of S_K.
3. Nothing else is a member of S_K.

If S_K is defined in this way, we shall say that it constitutes a *normative system with the basis K*. And we shall say that a norm is *valid in* a set K of norms if and only if it belongs to the normative system which is based on K. Thus, the norm N is valid in K if and only if $N \in S_K$. For example, the norm expressed by (14) is valid in any set of norms which contains the norm expressed by (13). We shall say, finally, that a norm *exists* or is *in force* if and only if it is valid in a set K of norms each one of which has been admitted in an act of decision and not subsequently rejected in a decision of type cancellation.

We observed in Section 8 that the consequence relationship $E_a q \models$

$E_a(q \vee r)$ does not hold. This means that R1 for Shall cannot be applied to yield Shall $E_a q \models$ Shall $E_a(q \vee r)$. Therefore, a normative system which contains the norm $(p \supset \text{Shall } E_a q)$ does not on that ground alone also contain the norm $(p \supset \text{Shall } E_a(q \vee r))$. In other words, Ross's Paradox does not hold for norms correlating simple one-agent normative positions and conditions or, as we might also say, it does not hold for simple one-agent norms. Accordingly, the paradox may not be used to make a normative system comprising such norms grow indefinitely in respect of the genuine tasks it prescribes. But it is true that the norm formulation $(p \supset \text{Shall } E_a q)$ implies the norm formulation $(p \supset \text{Shall}(E_a q \vee E_b r))$. Ross's Paradox may therefore be used to extend indefinitely a normative system which comprises complex 2-agent norms and, more generally, complex n-agent norms, but this use of the paradox is quite harmless because the states of affairs that are permitted under the norm $(p \supset \text{Shall}(E_a q \vee E_b r))$ in a normative system containing the norm $(p \supset \text{Shall } E_a q)$ do not warrant any conclusions as to b's obligation to bring about r. For reasons of space we cannot here substantiate this claim in detail.

We note that, on the suggested explication, the existence of a norm is clearly different from its enforcement, at least conceptually. And, as a matter of fact, not every norm that is in force in the sense explained, is enforced on every occasion of its violation, and, conversely, that which is enforced is usually, but not always, a norm in force. The correlation of norms with sanction, the central element in enforcement, is an empirical generalization, which is well-founded in the case of some communities and only a desired state of affairs in others. If one holds a 'realist' view of the nature of norms, it is tempting to make this correlation a defining feature of norm. This definitional use of the correlation can be given a high degree of systematic treatment and elaboration, as is evident from, for example, such works as Anderson (1956), and Pörn (1970). Here we have suggested an alternative, 'realist' conception, the focus of which is not on punitive reaction but on action (or reaction) of another sort, *viz*. decision, which is the term we use to cover the admission and rejection of norms.

If we allow some inaccuracy, we can express the circumstance that a believes that the norm expressed by (8) is valid in a set K of existing norms and, hence, that the norm is in force by writing

(15) $B_a((p \supset \text{Shall } E_a q) \in S_K)$.

It should be clear by now that this belief and that expressed by (9) are distinct. (15) is considerably more complex than (9) and, importantly, the two are logically independent of one another. It may be true that (9) implies that the norm (8) is in force, but this, clearly, need not be believed by a. Conversely, (15) does not imply (9). As we have already remarked, it is crucial for the assessment of our analysis of (7) that the difference between (9) and (15) be appreciated; the analysis is likely to appear widely unsound as a result of a failure to appreciate the difference.

15. INTENTIONAL ACTION

An existing norm such as (8) is *applicable* if and only if the condition p obtains. When the intention norm (8) exists, in which case (9) is true, it is applicable if and only if a believes that p is the case. Because F3 holds for belief it follows that a also believes that he should bring q about. It may be said here that p is a reason which a has for believing that he should bring q about. And when a has some reason for believing that he should bring it about that q it is the case that

(16) a intends to bring it about that q.

However, the applicability of a norm is one thing, its *application* another. It is the idea of application which must be elucidated if the action-guiding function of norms is to be understood. This goes for intentional action as well, for intentional action is the application of an intention. Under what circumstances is it true that a norm is applied?

The existence of a norm does not by itself issue in action, logically or causally. An agent may be subject to a norm, e.g. an expectation, without knowing this to be so; perhaps he was never informed, or perhaps he was informed but has now forgotten his task or the condition to which it is attached. In this sort of case the norm cannot influence the agent's action simply because there is no channel for its influence on him. In order for this to take place the agent must be aware of its existence and its applicability — believe that the norm exists and is applicable. But this is not sufficient. It is also necessary that the agent should translate his belief into action, or perform the task defined by the norm in the light of his conviction that it exists and is applicable.

We think that similar considerations are relevant in the case of intentions. In this case there is not the same information problem, for an intention is, by definition, a norm that is admitted to the beliefs of the agent whose intention it is. But even if this is granted, it does not follow that the fact that an agent intends to do an act by itself gives rise to the intended act. The agent may not believe that this intention is applicable, and therefore makes no attempt to apply the intention norm. Or if he does believe that the intention is applicable, he may refrain from application because he believes that the norm is not practicable in his present situation – a norm of type (8) is practicable in a situation, as described by a (finite) conjunction W, if and only if $M(W \& p \& E_a q)$. Or if he believes that it is practicable and makes an attempt to carry out his intention, he may fail because the norm is not in fact practicable. And even if the agent believes correctly that his applicable intention is practicable in his present situation and does the intended act, he need not act *on the ground of his intention*. However it is the last-mentioned factor which is required, if the intention is to have an action-guiding function and the action performed is to have the character of an intentional action. How, then, should this factor be understood?

If intentions do not by themselves determine the actions of the agents whose intentions they are, what does? To us, the short answer is: the agents themselves. We suggest that the action-guiding function of intentions is to be thought of in terms of the performance by intending agents of actions of a certain kind. In order for an intention to issue in action, *action* of type volition must intervene. We propose to speak of this as 'setting oneself to do' that which the intention prescribes and has selected as a task.

Setting oneself to do is a vague concept and cannot be used as a term of analysis unless the conditions of its use are defined. We propose to define these in the following way. First, a sets himself to bring it about that q on the condition that p only if

(17) $\qquad (B_a p \supset E_a q)$.

In other words, that which is expressed by (17) is necessary for something that a does. So if a sets himself to bring it about that q on the condition that p, then

(18) $\qquad D_a (B_a p \supset E_a q)$.

But it is also analytically true that if a sets himself to bring it about that q on the condition that p, then but for a's action it might be the case that a believes that p obtains but does not bring it about that q. That is

(19) $\qquad C'_a (B_a p \supset E_a q)$

is also true. By (Df3), the conjunction of (18) and (19) may be written as

(20) $\qquad E_a (B_a p \supset E_a q)$.

By our general solution to the characterization problem for action, (17) is an act description and expresses as such an action with a as agent if and only if it is equivalent to (20). The reading 'a brings it about that q if p' may be used for

(17) conceived of as an act description, but this reading is far from ideal since it may be used also when (17) is *not* so conceived. To disambiguate the matter we therefore propose to use the reading '*a* sets himself to bring it about that *q* on the condition that *p*' whenever (17) is thought of as an act description and, hence, as equivalent to (20). (A notion of setting oneself to do is used frequently in von Wright (1971, esp. Chapter 3), to indicate that 'behavior has been initiated' (p. 96). So used the notion is at least compatible, if not identical, with the sense we have given it.)

If *a* sets himself or has set himself to bring it about that *q* on the condition that *p*, and this condition is (believed by *a* to be) fulfilled, then we shall say that *a* brings it about that *q on the ground that p*. Deciding to do and setting oneself to do are structurally similar but materially dissimilar actions, and acting on some ground is obviously different from having an intention on some ground. In the latter case a task is grounded, whereas in the former case the actual bringing about of something is grounded on the fact that a condition is fulfilled.

Here one is tempted to bring in the notion of the will. Traditionally the will is the power by which the mind decides on an action. Acts of type decision are the immediate manifestations of an agent's will. We have distinguished between two types of decision — decisions in which intentions are formed and decisions in which (normative) expectations vis-à-vis the conduct of others are formed. In either case a belief is acquired by the agent making the decision. However, in the concept of the will one might also include the power by which the mind directs or controls the performance of an act when the act is done in the light of certain beliefs. These are, characteristically, an intention, i.e. the belief that the act shall be done on a condition and the belief that this condition is fulfilled. Deciding to act and setting oneself to act are actions of type volition.

The ground of an action may be a belief of any of a number of different kinds. Assume, however, that the ground is that the agent intends to do the action in question. *Then* the action is intentional, or so we shall say. In other words, we have now arrived at our explication of intentional action: *a* brings it about that *p* intentionally if and only if *a* brings it about that *p* on the ground that *a* intends to bring it about that *p*.

The central point of this explication does not seem to admit of debate. When we say that an agent does something intentionally we mean of course that he does it and that he has the intention to do it. But in addition we mean to say that the action is grounded on the intention. If this were not so, we would have lost sight of the main point of the reference to an intention — that it guides or controls action. And the problematic feature of the explication concerns the nature of that control, or the nature of the relation that the agent bears to himself when he does what he does because of or on the ground of his intention to do it. We take this relation to be a causal or, more precisely, an agent-causal relation. (In Chapter 6 we return to the question of the nature of the relation between intention and action, including the nature of the relation between intention and action in intentional action.) An agent who does what he does on the ground of his intention to do it has self-determination or self-control, which is the character of an agent who, as we would normally say, carries out his intention. It is this element of self-determination that we have tried to capture in terms of setting oneself to do as opposed to making a decision in the sense of forming or fixing one's intention.

16. TRANSMISSION OF INTENTION

According to common sense a primary intention to do an act, coupled with a belief concerning a means to that end, may induce the secondary intention to adopt the means. Assume, for instance, that

$$(9) \qquad B_a(p \supset \text{Shall } E_a q)$$

is exemplified thus: a intends to spend the long vacation in the country on the condition that he manages to install central heating in his country cottage before the beginning of the vacation. Assume also that a believes that if he manages to install central heating, then it is necessary for him to ask the bank for an advance, if he does spend the long vacation in the country. We may express this belief by

$$(21) \qquad B_a(p \supset N(E_a q \supset E_a r))$$

If a now also has the intention

$$(22) \qquad B_a(p \supset \text{Shall } E_a r)$$

and he has this not independently but because of the intention (9) and the belief (21), then we have a case of transmission of intention; let us call it Case 1. By Case 2 we shall understand the case where the *decision* to adopt the means is taken because of the intention (9) and the belief (21). Case 2 is thus like Case 1 except that

$$(23) \qquad E_a B_a(p \supset \text{Shall } E_a r)$$

takes the place of (22).

How should transmission of intention be understood? As regards Case 1, the suggestion might be that the word 'because' which occurs in our description of the case is used to signal that (22) is a logical consequence of (9) and (21). It is far from easy to see how this suggestion might be substantiated. The logic of L, as developed thus far, does not contain the consequence relationship in question. It would be in the logic of L, if the principle

(N.Shall) $(N(p \supset q) \supset (\text{Shall } p \supset \text{Shall } q))$

were also in the logic of L. For we would then have

$$(p \supset \text{Shall } E_a q), (p \supset N(E_a q \supset E_a r)) \models (p \supset \text{Shall } E_a r)$$

and principle R3, in Section 11, would yield the desired consequence relationship. But the semantics of L does not validate (N.Shall). We think that this is right and that (N.Shall) should be understood, not as a logical truth, but as a principle of another sort. What sort?

Assume that a set of tasks or jobs is believed by an agent to have the property expressed by (N.Shall). In other words, the agent believes that if q is a necessary means to p and p is a task in the set concerned, then the task q is also in the set. When structured in this way the set may be said to constitute a *project* according to the agent and depending on whether his belief is true or false the project may be said to be or not to be *well-ordered*. Not every set of tasks constitutes a project, and not every project is *well-ordered*. From the point of view of considerations such as these (N.Shall) can be seen to be true, not of all projects, which it would be if it was a logical truth, but only of well-ordered projects; it represents a defining feature of well-ordered projects and as such it formulates a kind of rationality requirement. When an intending agent believes that a set of intentions of his has the property expressed by (N.Shall) the set constitutes a project which is believed by him to be well-ordered. We could also describe the characteristic belief which gives his intentions unity and makes them constitute a project by saying that he believes that he is *practically consistent* (in certain respects) in his planning.

If the above argument is correct, it shows that the 'because' of our presentation of Case 1 does not refer to a logical consequence. This conclusion, however, is at variance with the intuition that it is not logically possible for a not to have the intention (22) given that he holds all the beliefs he is assumed to hold and that these are related in the way indicated. How should this be explained?

If the 'because' of our presentation of Case 1 does not refer to a logical consequence, it is a material component which should be made explicit in the analysis of the case. We get an intuitively very plausible analysis of Case 1, if we articulate it in the following way: $(p \supset \text{Shall } E_a q)$ and $(p \supset N(E_a q \supset E_a r))$ are in Case 1 *reasons* which a has for believing that $(p \supset \text{Shall } E_a r)$. The concept of reason exercised here is characterized by the condition that p is a reason which a has for believing that q if and only if a believes that if p then q and also believes that p. Thus, a reference to p as a reason which a has for believing that q is essentially an application of F3 for the concept of belief.

The application of this concept of reason in the suggested analysis of Case 1 allows us to see immediately how the material 'because' should be made explicit: it must be the belief expressed by

$$(24) \qquad B_a (((p \supset \text{Shall } E_a q) \& (p \supset N(E_a q \supset E_a r))) \supset (p \supset \text{Shall } E_a r))$$

in virtue of which the intention (9) and the belief (21) can appear as a's reasons for holding the belief (22). (24) expresses that a believes that a project of his is well-ordered or, which is the same, that he is practically consistent in his planning. But if (24) is a component of Case 1, then (22) is after all a logical consequence of the statement of other components of the case, for (9), (21), (24) $\models$ (22), which serves to justify the intuition that the correct analysis of Case 1 should reveal a relationship of logical consequence.

We next turn to Case 2. There are some important affinities between this and Case 1, but the story must be a little longer than in Case 1 for the intention (9) and the belief (21) cannot be a's reasons for holding the belief (23) simply because (23) does not express a belief but an action. They can constitute his reasons for believing that he should have the intention (22), however. This is the case if

$$(25) \qquad B_a (((p \supset \text{Shall } E_a q) \& (p \supset N(E_a q \supset E_a r))) \supset \text{Shall } B_a (p \supset \text{Shall } E_a r))$$

is true, in which case a believes, not that he is practically consistent, but that he should be. (9), (21), and (25) yield

$$(26) \qquad B_a \text{ Shall } B_a (p \supset \text{Shall } E_a r)$$

as a logical consequence. (26) expresses that a has a second-order intention. If a further believes that he is not going to have the first-order intention mentioned in (26) unless he forms it, in which case

$$(27) \qquad B_a N(B_a (p \supset \text{Shall } E_a r) \supset E_a B_a (p \supset \text{Shall } E_a r))$$

is true, and a also believes that this second-order project is well-formed, in which case

(28) $B_a((\text{Shall } B_a(p \supset \text{Shall } E_a r) \ \& \ N(B_a(p \supset \text{Shall } E_a r) \supset$
           $E_a B_a(p \supset \text{Shall } E_a r))) \supset \text{Shall } E_a B_a(p \supset \text{Shall } E_a r))$

is true, then a has reasons for believing that he should form the intention
and he has the intention to form it since (26)–(28) yield

(29) $B_a \text{ Shall } E_a B_a(p \supset \text{Shall } E_a r)$

as a logical consequence. If, finally, a forms the intention on the ground of
this intention, then

(30) $E_a(B_a \text{ Shall } E_a B_a(p \supset \text{Shall } E_a r) \supset E_a B_a(p \supset \text{Shall } E_a r))$

is true and (23) follows.

Since (23) logically implies (22), it may be said that in Case 2, as in Case
1, an intention is derived. But this must not be allowed to blur the distinction
between the two cases and the difference between having reasons for
believing and acting on the ground of an intention for which one has reasons.
To make the difference we shall say that an intention is *derived* in Case 1 and
evolved in Case 2, and when the difference happens to be immaterial for the
purposes at hand we shall speak of the transmission or transfer of intention
and use the compendious 'because'. The derivation and evolution of intentions may be compared with the following well-known aspects of law: the
lawyer's concern to know and analyse the law, and the legislator's concern to
evolve the law through some act of legal change.

In our discussion above of transmission of intention we have spoken only
of necessary means. Similar considerations apply, and parallel logical
structures are forthcoming, in the case of transmission which turns on
sufficient means or means which are both necessary and sufficient. We shall
not stop to review the details here.

17. ACTING WITH A FURTHER INTENTION

We have explicated the notion of an intention to perform an action, the
notion of intentional action and the notion of transmission of intention.
There remains the notion of performing an action with the intention of
performing some other action. No new conceptual ingredients are required to
cope with this case, for 'a brings it about that p with the intention of bringing
it about that q' is true if and only if the following two conditions are satisfied:
a intends to bring about p because a intends to bring about q and, secondly,
a brings about p intentionally. Acting with a further intention is thus a
comparatively complex constellation of factors involving, as it does, transmis-

sion of intention and intentional action. (Acting with a further intention is the pattern of thought and action which is studied in von Wright (1971), under the heading 'the practical syllogism (inference)'. See also von Wright (1972).)

18. REASONS FOR ACTION AND WANTS

An agent has a reason for an action if and only if he has a reason for believing that he should perform this action or, equivalently, has a reason for intending to perform it. If he performs it on the ground of this intention, he may be said to perform the action for a reason, *viz*. the reason he has for intending to perform it. Since he can have many reasons for an intention – many reasons for holding the belief that constitutes his intention – an action done on the ground of this intention may be an action done for many reasons. Multiple reasons are given the unity of one purpose in an intention and are present in one and the same action via this intention.

According to the above characterization an action done for a reason is always also an intentional action. We have already implied that the converse is also true, for we have said that an agent intends an action if and only if he intends to do it on some condition which is believed by him to be fulfilled; this condition is then a reason which the agent has for doing the action and if he does act on the ground of his intention, his action is done for reasons which include the condition. An intentional action is therefore also an action done for a reason. Thus, by our conception, an action is intentional if and only if it is done for a reason. The truth of this equivalence, however, does not mean that an intentional action and an action done for a reason are conceptually identical.

In the category of reasons for action *wants* occupy a prominent place. One interesting hypothesis in that one of the reasons an agent always has when he acts intentionally is that he wants a state of affairs. Before we try to elucidate this conception more directly we shall consider the concept of wanting itself.

The basic element in the concept of wanting seems to be the deontic modality Ought ('It ought to be the case that') used in an evaluative sense. To indicate this sense we could also read a wff of the kind Ought p as 'It is an optimum that p' or 'it is optimal that p'. When Ought is used in the evaluative sense Ought p is to the effect that p is true of that alternative which is better in some respect than any other alternative that is available in a given situation or, if there be a class of such maximal alternatives between which no relevant value discrimination can be made, then Ought p means that p is true of each maximal alternative. So if we understand the idealization relation R(Ought) in such a way that $(u, v) \in R(\text{Ought})$ if and only if v is first in rank among the relevant alternatives available in u, in which case v may be said to be a deontic ideal of u, then we may use (OM1) for the truth-value determination of a wff of the kind Ought p. It is natural to assume that $R(\text{Ought})$ is serial in U of a model $\mathcal{M} = (U, R, M, M')$. Given this, R1, R2, F2, F3, F5—F8, and F11 hold for Ought.

Ought in the evaluative sense and Shall are distinct notions. The latter connects with action of type decision in a way which has already been articulated. That which is or has been decided plainly need not be superior in preference, nor is it the case that a state of affairs that is superior in preference is always fixed in a decision. The two notions are therefore independent in the sense that Ought p neither implies nor is implied by Shall p. The only logical connection between them seems to be that a prescription can be characterized as an optimum only if that which is prescribed can be so characterized, i.e.

(31)   (Ought Shall $p \supset$ Ought p)

is a logical truth. As observed by Kanger (1972, p. 121), the corresponding model condition is that $R(\text{Ought})$ be a subset of the relative product $R(\text{Ought})/R(\text{Shall})$.

As our model of a want we shall take the belief that a state of affairs is an optimum. That is to say, we shall read $B_a \text{Ought } p$ as 'a wants that p (be the case)'. This idea will receive elaboration in the next section. Here we return to the hypothesis that one of the reasons for which an agent acts when he performs an intentional action is a want. This is, more precisely, a thesis concerning the intelligibility of projects and their execution.

Consider an intention complex which is a project because it is structured in the following way: the agent intends to bring p about because he intends to bring q about, he intends to bring q about because he intends to bring r about, and so on. Having an intention simpliciter may be considered the limiting case of a project and intentional action the limiting case of the execution of a project. With respect to all members of a project or its execution except the last member the question 'Why does the agent intend to do this?' or, alternatively, 'Why does the agent do that?' may be answered in terms of the intention to perform the next member. But there is also, without any doubt, a why-question concerning the last member of a project or its execution and this cannot, *ex hypothesi*, be answered in the same way. How, then, should *it* be answered? According to the hypothesis referred to above, only the specification of the reasons which the agent has for the last intention, or the reasons for which he acts when he carries it out, can count as an answer and, secondly and importantly, this must include the specification of something wanted or thought best by the agent. The hypothesis may therefore be formulated in the following way: in a project or its execution the agent always intends, ultimately and perhaps also more immediately, an action the reasons for which include a state of affairs wanted (thought best) by him. We shall accept this hypothesis and refer to it as the *principle of ideality*.

This principle should not be confused with the different idea that an intention task is always something one really wants to carry out, i.e. the thesis that $(B_a \text{Shall } p \supset B_a \text{Ought } p)$. This is not always true. A wanted state of affairs and the circumstance that its realization requires an action may be reasons which an agent has for doing the action without it being the case that he wants to do it: the inference

(32)
$$
\begin{array}{ll}
\text{(i)} & B_a \text{ Ought } p \\
\text{(ii)} & B_a \text{N}(p \supset E_a q) \\
\text{(iii)} & \underline{B_a((\text{Ought } p \ \& \ \text{N}(p \supset E_a q)) \supset \text{Shall } E_a q)} \\
\text{(iv)} & B_a \text{ Ought } E_a q
\end{array}
$$

is not valid. (i)–(iii) yield the intention conclusion $B_a \text{ Shall } E_a q$, but not the want statement (iv).

The principle of ideality is of course satisfied in a situation described by (i)–(iii): in any such situation a wanted state of affairs is among the reasons which the agent has for the intended action. Indeed, the structure of (i)–(iii), which yield the conclusion $B_a \text{ Shall } E_a q$, gives a clue to one way in which the principle of ideality might be made more precise:

Principle of ideality. If an agent does not want to do an action q which he intends to do, then a state of affairs p wanted by him and the circumstance that $(\text{N}(p \supset r_1) \ \& \ \text{N}(r_1 \supset r_2) \ \& \ ... \ \& \text{N}(r_n \supset q))$, for $n \geqslant 1$, are reasons which he has for doing the intended action.

In the sequel we shall presuppose the principle of ideality in this form.

From (i) and (ii) of (32) the want conclusion (iv) follows if

(v) $B_a(\text{N}(p \supset E_a q) \supset (\text{Ought } p \supset \text{Ought } E_a q))$

is also true. A wanted state of affairs and the circumstance that its realization requires an action are then reasons which the agent has for wanting to do the action. The belief held by a in case (v) is an instance of the principle

(N.Ought) $(\text{N}(p \supset q) \supset (\text{Ought } p \supset \text{Ought } q))$

which says that a necessary condition of an ideal state of affairs is itself ideal. (N.Ought) is not valid. It plays a role in the transmission of wants which is analogous to that of (N.Shall) in the transmission of intentions. In other words, it is a synthetic principle which is operative when wants are transmitted from one state of affairs to another, in some cases via a want to have an intention, in which cases (31) is involved.

19. VALUATIONS AND VALUE POSITIONS

A want, understood in the indicated general sense, may be coupled with the belief that there is nothing one can do to realize the optimum. Then the want is merely an idle wish. Or it may be coupled with the conviction that the optimum is realizable without any action being done for the reason of the want. Then the want is a velleity. Or it may be a reason for which some action is done. Then it gives rise to the 'endeavour toward' the thing wanted or the 'endeavour fromward' the thing unwanted which since Hobbes has often been thought of as a characteristic feature of wanting. It will not be necessary for our present purposes thus to distinguish cases according to the nature of the context in which a want in our general sense occurs.

The structure we have suggested for a positive desire is obviously just one member of a very large class of structures. We shall say that all of these express valuations and we will now show how some subclasses of valuations may be defined. We believe that the concept of a valuation and the closely related concept of a value position may be used to elucidate the notion of an attitude, which occupies a central place in sociological theory.

Value positions are defined in terms of Ought and standard logical means. A sentence of the form Ought p expresses a value position, and so do sentences of the form Ought$\sim p$ or the form $\sim$Ought$\sim p$. We are inclined to express the last-mentioned value position by saying that it is good that p. In other words, we are inclined to accept the definition

(Df16)   Good $p = \sim$Ought$\sim p$.

By using a method like that employed in the theory of normative positions it is possible to build a theory of valuations and value positions. Consider

	(i)	Ought p
(33)	(ii)	Ought$\sim p$
	(iii)	$\sim$(Ought p v Ought$\sim p$).

It is plain that the disjunction of (i)–(iii) is complete and exhaustive. By

replacing Shall by B_a we can give (33) a role similar to that of (5) to obtain a
list analogous to (6). We have:

(34.		1	2	3	4	5	6	7)
B_a Ought p		+	−	−	−	−	−	−
$B_a \sim$Ought p		−	+	+	+	−	−	−
B_a Ought$\sim p$		−	+	−	−	−	−	−
$B_a \sim$Ought$\sim p$		+	−	+	−	+	−	−
$B_a \sim$(Ought p ∨ Ought$\sim p$)		−	−	+	−	−	−	−
B_a (Ought p ∨ Ought$\sim p$)		+	+	−	−	−	+	−

The consistent conjunction (1)–(7) express *valuations* in contradistinction to
(i)–(iii), which express *value positions*. (The procedure described on page 23,
with reference to Lindahl (1977), can be applied to yield a list equivalent to
(34). The dual of B_a, which perhaps may be read in terms of acquiescence,
has the properties necessary for the application of the procedure.) The
distinction concerns in the first instance only beliefs of a certain kind and
their contents. We are not saying that the distinction is radical in the sense
that it is possible to define value positions without resorting to the notion of
belief. In the previous section the truth conditions of wffs of the kind· Ought
p were stated in terms of the truth-value of p in ideal versions of a given
world. It is virtually certain that such ideal versions can be defined independently of beliefs actually held by agents or persons. It is doubtful, however,
whether they can be defined independently of the beliefs that persons would
hold in certain hypothetical situations, say situations in which they are fully
informed of all relevant factors.

The type structure of valuations is exceedingly rich. (1)–(7) yield the
basic types of simple valuations and the use of set operations in this area
will yield the corresponding non-basic types. For example, the union of type
4 and type 6 is a complex type of simple valuation; it may be termed non-
indifference in view of the fact that a subject who holds a valuation of this
type wants either a state of affairs or its opposite to be the case. Complex
valuations and their types may be studied given the joint assertions of two or
more disjunctions of the form (33).

This is not the end, however. There is a distinction between *orders* of
valuations which quickly increases the complexity of the type structure for
valuations. When p in (i)–(iii) of (33) does not express a valuation (1)–(7) of
(34) express first-order valuations or valuations of the first order. When p in
(i)–(iii) does express a valuation (1)–(7) express valuations of a higher order.
(The distinction between valuations and metavaluations appears to have been

first introduced in Stenius (1955), reprinted in Stenius (1972).) If we treat p in (i)–(iii) as a variable ranging over (1)–(7), we have 3×7 or 21 starter elements. Since B_a and $\sim B_a$ may be appended to each of these, we get an initial list of 2^{21} conjunctions. Not all of these are consistent; it is in fact possible to reduce the number of conjunctions considerably by removing the inconsistent lists. We shall not now stop to discuss this reduction.

Higher-order valuations are very common. To illustrate, let p be the sentence 'a smokes about 20 cigarettes a day'. a's valuation of his own smoking might well include the following wants:

$$B_a \text{ Ought } p$$
$$B_a \text{ Ought} \sim B_a \text{ Ought } p$$
$$B_a \text{ Ought} \sim B_a \text{ Ought} \sim B_a \text{ Ought } p.$$

That is to say, a has the first-order desire to smoke about 20 cigarettes a day, the second-order desire to be rid of his first-order desire to smoke about 20 a day, and the third-order desire to be rid of his second-order desire to be rid of his first-order desire. Cases involving desires of higher order than three occur and can easily be imagined.

20. ATTITUDES

Attitude studies are a central concern in social psychology. There are good reasons why the study of attitudes should be prominent. A process of socialization terminates with the formation of an attitude and attitudes, once formed, operate in combination with factors of other kinds as determinants of action.

The concept of attitude is normally regarded as a three-dimensional construct. An attitude, it is often said, has an affective, a cognitive, and a conative aspect. Under this conception an attitude is a very complex constellation of factors, so complex, in fact, that the term tends to become a blanket term used to refer to any act disposition together with its set of motives however complex. The usefulness of the three-dimensional notion as a tool of empirical research has been questioned, and then an alternative suggestion is made in favour of the introduction of a simpler, unidimensional concept to refer to the affect for or against some psychological object. (See esp. Fishbein (1965, 1966).) From our point of view this theoretical simplification, which seems desirable, may naturally be articulated as follows.

Just as a norm correlates a normative position and a condition, so an attitude may be said to correlate a value position and a condition. Thus, if we interpret $Tq(x)$ of (2) as the expression of a value position, (2) may be taken as the most general form of formulations or statements of attitudes, while (3) and (4) are slightly simpler forms of attitude statements. 'Sex education ought to be given at school to all boys and girls' and 'A child should never keep a secret from his parents' are two simple examples of attitude statements of form (2). In the first example, 'x is a boy or a girl' expresses the attitude restriction and 'x is at school' the attitude condition. The distinction between the restriction and the condition of an attitude is helpful in some contexts, e.g. if we wish to distinguish between a person's attitude to negroes as workmates and his attitude to negroes as neighbours. If we do not distinguish between the two components, the attitude in our first example may be expressed by a statement of the form

(35) $\forall x(p(x) \supset \text{Ought } q(x))$

A person a has the attitude if and only if he is convinced of its truth, in which case

(36) $B_a \forall x(p(x) \supset \text{Ought } q(x))$

is true; attitudes, like intentions, have only notional existence. And, like norms, attitudes can be grouped into sets and systems. An attitude may or may not be valid in a set of attitudes; if it is, it belongs to the attitude system which is based on the set concerned. There are thus far-reaching affinities between the theoretical treatment of norms and that of attitudes.

The suggested explication of the concept of an attitude enables us immediately to articulate questions concerning the relationship between attitudes and other phenomena, such as valuations, factual beliefs, intentions, and actions. The conjunction of (36) and

(37) $B_a \forall_x(r(x) \supset p(x))$

implies the attitude statement

(38) $B_a \forall_x(r(x) \supset \text{Ought } q(x))$

The conjunction of (38) and $\exists x \, B_a(x = b)$ or $B_a \exists x(x = b)$ implies

(39) $B_a(r(b) \supset \text{Ought } q(b))$

which expresses a singular attitude. In virtue of this a's belief that $r(b)$, if actually held by a, is a reason which a has for taking up the value position Ought $q(b)$. Hence, attitudes may be derived from other attitudes via factual beliefs and when embedded in suitable belief sets they yield valuations. These may in turn serve as reasons for having certain intentions, i.e. they may serve as reasons for actions. Our principle of ideality may be seen as a conjecture about the kind of relationship which may obtain between attitudes and behavioural intentions. Finally, in order for an attitude to 'determine' action it is further necessary that an intention derived from some valuation of the attitude, or an intention transmitted from an intention so derived, be applied in an intentional action. From the logical point of view the organization of actions in terms of attitudes is an exceedingly complex affair.

CHAPTER 3

ACTIVITIES AND PROCEEDINGS

Actions may be grouped into wholes which exhibit a definite structure. Such structured wholes are here termed action complexes, and in this chapter our main concern is to study the nature and structure of action complexes. Actions performed by individual agents are regarded as units at the basic level. The complexes built up of such units are subdivided into activities and proceedings. An attempt is made to describe such complexes in terms drawn from the theory of grammars and automata.

21. ACTION COMPLEXES

Actions may be distinguished into simple and complex. Act relations and their instances constitute the class of simple actions. We shall subdivide action complexes into activities and proceedings. By an *activity* we understand a sequence of actions, and, in the last analysis, a sequence of simple actions. The components of an activity are regarded as simultaneous but, since they are components of a sequence, ordered in some other way. For example, closing a window by pressing a lever is an activity and so is pressing a lever by closing a window. These two activities are distinct because the sets concerned are different ordered sets. In these examples only one agent is involved, but there are of course activities which involve two or more agents. For example, the complex action exhibited when two persons shake hands with each other is an activity involving two agents.

By a *proceeding* we shall understand a temporally ordered sequence of activities. First to remove the screws that retain a lid and then to remove the lid is a proceeding, which may involve more than one agent, and so is the complex action exhibited when two persons shake hands with each other, then exchange civil remarks and conclude their encounter by saying good-bye.

Notice that a simple action may have three characters: one when regarded merely as a simple action, another when regarded as an activity consisting of just one simple action, and a third when regarded as a one-element sequence of activities.

In the analysis of activities and proceedings with more than one agent there is perhaps some temptation to regard groups of acting individuals as unitary agents. According to this suggestion a predicate like '*a* and *b* shake hands', or 'a and b shake hands and then quarrel', should be understood as an agent-causal predicate with a collective agent index, *viz*. the list 'a and b'. This idea, however, does not seem to be very satisfactory. It tends to conceal altogether the problem under consideration: we are not helped in our concern to understand the structure and integration of complex behaviour by the suggestion that groups can appear as unitary agents, for an important aspect of the problem is to understand how the action of a group is related to the actions of the individual contributors. In the sequel we shall try to maintain the suggested distinction between simple and complex action without resorting to predicates with collective agent indices. We shall do this by showing that the structure of complex action can be understood without the use of such predicates.

22. STRUCTURE OF ACTIVITIES: TWO EXAMPLES

The structure of a complex action, whether activity or proceeding, is due to such factors as the number of agents involved, the circumstances that attend the component actions, and the results or consequences that these produce. To form a clearer perception of this we consider two examples illustrating how a definite structure is imposed on an activity by attendant circumstances and results produced.

A man uses a lead pipe to convey water from one place to another. It is true of him that he introduces metallic poison into the water, if the water happens to contain dissolved air. In other words, given this state of the water, the man introduces metallic poison into the water by the use of a lead pipe for its transportation. That his activity has this structure or character — that it is an instance of introducing metallic poison into the water by the use of a lead pipe for its transportation — is due to the state of the water, an attendant circumstance, and to a definite result or consequence, *viz*. the formation of metallic poison. We may say that his activity has the structure it has because the agent in performing it manipulates a deterministic system or automaton, the operative feature of which is the natural necessity that the exposure of lead to air results in the formation of the soluble hydroxide, which is poisonous.

In our second example we make more explicit use of the notion of an automaton. Consider the automaton represented in Table II. The table describes the way in which the switch of an electric light works. If the ciruit is open at time t and the position of the button is altered at $t + 1$, then the circuit is closed at $t + 1$, in which case the light is on; if, on the

TABLE II

Tabular description of an automaton

	light is on	light is off
	circuit is closed	circuit is open
position of button is altered	circuit is open	circuit is closed

other hand, the circuit is closed at t and the position of the button is altered at $t + 1$, then the circuit is open at $t + 1$, in which case the light is off.

In the language of the theory of automata, the system may be described thus: there is one input (alteration of the position of the switch button), two internal states (circuit closed, circuit open), two outputs (light on, light off), a next-state or transition function which sets out the changes of the internal states relative to the input the machine is receiving, and an output function which correlates an output with a state.

An agent operates this automaton by imposing an instance of the input, i.e. by altering the position of the button in the sense of bringing it about that the position of the button is altered. He thereby also turns on or off the light (depending on whether the circuit was open or closed before) in the sense of bringing it about that the light is on or off. In other words, the agent alters the position of the button and, at the same time, he turns the light on or off because of the working of the machine. His action at the time is a complex one, an activity, which is an instance of turning the light on or off by altering the position of the button. And that his action is an activity with this structure is due to the fact that in performing it the agent provides the input of a machine which transmits his agent-causality to an output. The complex action of the agent in our first example may obviously be analysed in the same way. However, before we discuss these and cognate ideas in greater generality, we shall introduce some elements from the theory of automata. (Salomaa (1969), gives a self-contained presentation of the theory of automata.)

23. FINITE AUTOMATA

An alphabet is a non-empty set of elements called letters. A word over the alphabet I is a finite sequence of letters of I. For example, from the alphabet $I = (0,1)$ the words $0,1,00,01,10,11,000, ...$ can be formed. Thus a word p over I exhibits a first position, a second position, and so on, up to an nth position. Here the integer n is a measure of the length $lg(p)$ of p and it is equal to the number of occurrences of letters of I in p. The word p such that

$lg(p) = 0$, i.e. the empty sequence over an alphabet, is called the empty word and written λ.

If p and q are words over I of lengths m and n, respectively, then their catenation pq is a word over I of length $m + n$. If $p = q$, the catenation pq may be written p^2 and, generally, if we set $p^0 = \lambda$ and $p^{n+1} = p^n p$, we may use p^n ($n \geqslant 0$) to denote the result of catenating n copies of the word p.

The set of all words over I is denoted $W(I)$. Any subset of $W(I)$ constitutes a language over I. If the letters of I are act relations, I is a *repertoire*. A word over a repertoire is an action complex, which is an activity or a proceeding depending on how the order of the letters in the word is defined.

As indicated in the previous section a finite automaton is a system A = $(I, O, S, f, \emptyset)$ where I, O, and S are finite, non-empty sets, f is a function from $S \times I$ into S, and $\emptyset$ a function from $S \times I$ into O. The sets I and O are the input and the output alphabet, respectively. S is the set of (internal) states, f the next-state (transition) function, and $\emptyset$ the output function. One interpretation of A is that it is a system which, if in state s at time t and receiving input p at time $t + 1$, will at time $t + 1$ be in state $f(s, p)$ and have output $\emptyset(s, p)$. Another interpretation is that A is a system which, if in state s at t and receiving input p at $t + 1$, will at $t + 1$ be in state $f(s, p)$ and have output $\emptyset(s, p)$ at $t + 2$.

An automaton of the general sort just defined is termed a (deterministic) sequential Mealy machine. Machines of many other types may be characterized by specialization of elements in the definition of a Mealy machine. Thus, a pair (A, s) where A is a Mealy machine and s is a distinguished state, called the initial state, is an initial Mealy machine. Some automata have the convenient and simplifying property that all transitions entering a given internal state have the same output. In this case the output function can be defined as $\emptyset(s, p) = U(f(s, p))$ where, clearly, U is a single-valued function from S to O. Such a system is called a sequential Moore machine. The table used in the second example of the previous section represents a sequential Moore machine.

If in a Moore machine the sets O and S coincide and U is the identity function, i.e. $U(s) = s$ for every s in $S(= O)$, the set O and the function U may be disregarded so that we are left with a system A = (I, S, f), called an automaton without outputs. Table III defines the transition function of an automaton without outputs and, *a fortiori*, the automaton whose transition function it is, for, obviously, $I = \{p_1, p_2\}$ and $S = \{s_0, s_1, s_2, s_3\}$ for the automaton concerned.

TABLE III

Transition function of an automaton without outputs

f	s_0	s_1	s_2	s_3
p_1	s_0	s_1	s_2	s_3
p_2	s_1	s_2	s_3	s_3

The transition function of an automaton is first defined for the input alphabet. It may be extended to cover the set of words over the alphabet in the following way:

$$f(s, \lambda) = s \quad \text{for all} \quad s \in S$$
$$f(s, Pp) = f(f(s, P), p) \quad \text{for all} \quad s \in S, P \in W(I), p \in I$$

For example, if the automaton just defined receives the input *word* $p_1 p_1 p_2$ and it is in the state s_0, it will go to state s_1 as the following calculation shows:

$$f(s_0, p_1 p_1 p_2) = f(f(s_0, p_1 p_1), p_2) = f(f(f(s_0, p_1), p_1), p_2) =$$
$$f(f(s_0, p_1), p_2) = f(s_0, p_2) = s_1$$

Thus a machine of the general sort defined above undergoes a sequence of changes in state under a sequence of inputs and produces a sequence of outputs. Hence the name 'sequential machine'. The behaviour of the machine is defined for discrete moments only. This means that its behaviour between these moments is not thought to bring in any new factors that are important for the understanding of the machine or else that it has no behaviour between the discrete moments.

Automata are often used as recognition devices. The main idea here is easily introduced and illustrated. Let $A = (I, S, f)$ be an automaton without outputs, let $s_0 \in S$ be the initial state, and let $S_1 \subseteq S$ be a set of distinguished states called the final states. We then have a finite-state acceptor. The name is justified for the system may be said to accept or recognize an input word P if and only if, given P and starting from the initial state, it reaches a final state, i.e. if and only if $f(s_0, P) \in S_1$. The set of all input words recognized in this way is the language accepted by the acceptor. We obtain a finite-state acceptor if, in the example above, we let s_0 be the intitial state and s_3 the (only) final state. This recognition device may be described by the following transition graph:

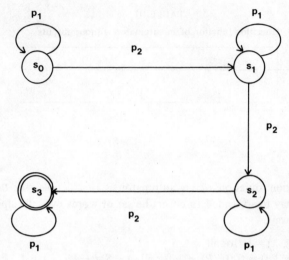

Fig. 1.   Transition graph of a finite-state acceptor.

We obtain an action interpretation of the device by letting p_1 be the act relation expressed by 'x lifts hammer y' and let p_2 be the act relation expressed by 'x strikes the head of a nail with hammer y', and by further letting the states be four positions of a nail and s_3 the position of the nail when its head is flush with the surface of a wall. Under this interpretation our finite-state acceptor recognizes all proceedings over the input repertoire which results in s_3. Since we have here another instance of the transmission of agency – a phenomenon we met in the two examples of the previous section – we may characterize the accepted language as the set of all proceedings of hammering a nail into a wall by lifting a hammer and striking the head of the nail with the hammer.

24. TRANSMISSION OF AGENCY

The structure of the cases that we have discussed, so far, by means of examples may be defined as follows. There is an automaton A such that $q = \mathcal{O}(s, p)$ for some state s, some input p, and some output (state) q. An agent operates A by bringing p about. On this basis we assert that the agent also brings q about. Under what conditions, it may be asked, is this assertion warranted? We next answer this question.

Assume that $q = \mathcal{O}(s, p)$ is true of some automaton A and also that $E_a p$ is true but $E_a q$ false in some situation u. The latter means (i) that $\sim D_a q$ is true in u or (ii) that $\sim C'_a q$ is true in u. In case (i) q is false in some situation u' such that everything that a does in u is the case in u'. By assumption $E_a p$ is true in u. It follows that p is true in u'. From this and the assumption that $q = \emptyset(s, p)$ we cannot conclude that q is true in u' to make case (i) inconsistent, for the assumptions are silent about the state s. However, if we introduce $D_a s$ as an additional assumption, then and only then is case (i) inconsistent.

In case (ii) q is true in every situation u' in which everything that a does in u, including the operation of A, is absent. This, of course, is quite conceivable – s might be present in u' and, if so, q might be the case because some other agent operates A or because q is the output of an automaton different from A. On the other hand, if case (ii) is made inconsistent by assumption, then one answer to the question before us takes the form

(1) $\forall A \forall s \in S_A((q = \emptyset_A (s, p) \ \& \ E_a p \ \& \ D_a s \ \& \ C'_a q) \supset E_a q)$.

We shall use the notation $E_a (p, q)$ to express the circumstance that the antecedent of the implication in (1) is fulfilled for some automaton A. That is to say, we introduce

(Df17) $E_a(p, q) = \exists \, A \, \exists \, s \in S_A (q = \emptyset_A (s, p) \ \& \ E_a p \ \& \ D_a s \ \& \ C'_a q)$

and read $E_a (p, q)$ as 'a brings it about that q by bringing it about that p'. For an illustration we can use one of the examples given in Section 22. According to (Df17) a introduces metallic poison into a volume of water by making the water flow through a lead pipe if and only if each of the following conditions is fulfilled: first, there is an automaton such that if the water contains dissolved air (s) and it flows through a lead pipe (p), then metallic poison is present in the water (q); second, a operates the automaton in respect of p, i.e. a makes the volume of water flow through a lead pipe; third, it is necessary for something which a does that the water contains dissolved air; and fourth, metallic poison might not have been present in the water, as and when it was present, but for the action or intervention of a. (Goldman (1970), is an interesting study, with resources different from ours, of the transmission of agency or 'generation' as Goldman calls it. Note, in particular, the use of this notion that is made in the recursive definition of the class of act-tokens.)

(1) calls for some comments. First, it makes fairly precise the intuitive idea that actions take on colour from the circumstances that attend them and from the outcomes. We think of the circumstances as the internal state of an automaton. We think of the operation of the automaton as action which provides an input and thus determines what the input is at a certain time. And we think of the outcome under consideration as an output of the automaton. The agency involved in the operation of the automaton is trans-

mitted to the output provided that the necessity condition and the counter-action condition above are fulfilled. Whenever there is transmission of agency, in this sense, a complex action arises. We describe the character and structure of this action complex by specifying the nature of the automaton and how it is operated.

Second, the result can be generalized recursively via the extension of the output function. This function is defined in the first instance as a function from $S \times I$ into O. It may be extended to a function from $S \times W(I)$ into O in the following way:

$$\emptyset(s, \lambda) = \lambda \text{ for all } s \in S$$
$$\emptyset(s, pP) = \emptyset(s, p)\emptyset(f(s, p), P) \text{ for all } s \in S, p \in I, P \in W(I).$$

Generalizations of this sort raise some interesting issues concerning the notions of result and consequence of action, but as these are not of any immediate relevance to our present concerns we shall not stop to consider the details here.

Third, since $|=(((p \supset q) \& p) \supset q)$ there clearly is an automaton A such that $q = \emptyset_A((p \supset q), p)$. In view of the fact that $E_a p$ implies $(E_a p \& D_a(p \supset p) \& C'_a p)$ it therefore follows that

$$\exists A(p = \emptyset_A((p \supset p), p) \& E_a p \& D_a(p \supset p) \& C'_a p)$$

if it is true that $E_a p$, i.e. $(E_a p \supset E_a(p, p))$ is valid. Since the converse is also valid we have

(2) $(E_a p \equiv E_a(p, p))$.

This means that in addition to the transmission thesis (1) for agency we have a transmission thesis in the form

(3) $(E_a p \equiv \exists q E_a(q, p))$.

Without (2) the assertion of (3) would immediately be rendered open to the charge of entailing an infinite regress. If p in (3) is of the form $E_a p$ we have

(4) $(E_a p \equiv \exists q E_a(q, E_a p))$

as a special case since $|=(E_a p \equiv E_a E_a p)$. (4) asserts a form of determinism for agency. We shall elaborate on this remark in the next section. ((3) and (4) are examples of formulae which belong to the modal second-order language $\mathscr{L}$ which was mentioned in Section 1.)

It is evident that

(5) $\forall A \forall s \in S_A((q = \emptyset_A(s, p) \& E_a p \& s \& C'_a q) \supset F_a q)$

holds. We shall use the notation $F_a(p, q)$ to express the circumstance that the antecedent of the implication in (5) is fulfilled for some automaton A. As a parallel to (Df17) we therefore introduce

(Df18) $F_a(p, q) = \exists A \exists s \in S_A (q = \emptyset_A(s, p) \,\&\, E_a p \,\&\, s \,\&\, C_a' q)$

and read $F_a(p, q)$ as 'from the fact that a brings it about that p it follows that q'.

$F_a(p, q)$ implies $F_a q$ but not $E_a q$. Further, $E_a(p, q)$ implies but is not implied by $F_a(p, q)$. The latter is therefore not relevant to the analysis of transmission of agency as we have tried to articulate it in this section. It is relevant, however, at least in those cases where q is an action and we shall return to these in our discussion of interaction in Chapter 4 and in our discussion of dynamic aspects of action in Chapter 5.

25. DETERMINISM AND AGENCY

Consider the class O^* of modalities O such that R1, F1, and

(6) $(E_a p \supset {\sim} Op)$

all hold for O. O^* is not empty. Universal necessity, understood as truth at every $u \in U$, belongs to O^*, and so do the modalities N_a, N, and I_a. And, of course, there are modalities which do not belong to O^*, e.g. E_b and F_b (irrespective of whether or not $a = b$) and D_a.

It can easily be shown that bringing something about, and, hence, the performance of an action, cannot be necessary, if 'necessary' is understood as referring to a modality in O^*. For assume $OE_a p$ for some $O \in O^*$. Then Op follows by R1 since $E_a p \mid= p$. But $OE_a p$ implies $E_a p$ by F1, and $E_a p$ implies ${\sim} Op$ by (6). Hence $OE_a p$ is self-inconsistent, i.e. ${\sim} OE_a p$ for every $O \in O^*$.

This result is relevant for the appraisal of determinism. Determinism is a cluster of theses, many of which are obscure and therefore difficult to assess for truth or plausibility. It is trivially true that if something happens of necessity, it follows that it happens. A thesis of determinism, if it is to be non-trivial, must, it seems, assert the converse, *viz.* that if something happens, if follows that it happens of necessity. In other words, a thesis of determinism worth the name must assert

(7) $(p \supset Op)$

for some notion O of necessity. The argument above shows that, if this notion is an O^*-necessity, then (7) implies ${\sim} E_a p$, for (7) yields $(E_a p \supset OE_a p)$

as a special case, but in view of the fact that $\sim OE_a p$ for every $O \in O^*$, $\sim E_a p$ follows. In other words, if (7) is true for some $O \in O^*$, then nobody ever brings anything about. Conversely, if one is convinced, as we are, that agency occurs, any thesis of determinism which asserts (7) for some $O \in O^*$ must be rejected. However, this does not preclude determinism from the world of agency altogether. Indeed, it follows from (Df9) that if p in (7) expresses an action with a as agent, then (7) holds in the form $(p \supset E_a p)$. There is therefore a form of determinism which is not only compatible with agency but also constituted by agency; in the world of agency a form of determinism is supplied by the agents themselves.

It might be said, alternatively, that a thesis of determinism worth the name must assert

(8) $(p \supset \exists q \; \exists A \; \exists s \in S_A \, (p = \emptyset_A (s, q)))$.

If so, the above argument shows two things: first, that the operation of an automaton by an agent cannot be necessary, in the sense of an O^*-necessity; and, second, that no automaton can transmit agency in such a way as to make the performance of an action necessary in that sense. But, again, these results do not mean that determinism is incompatible with agency. (4), for example, clearly implies a form of determinism which is compatible with agency, for it asserts that a brings p about if and only if a supplies an input element of a deterministic system and in so doing brings p about. Hence, certainly, (3) implies (8) in the form

(9) $(E_a p \supset \exists q \, \exists A \, \exists s \in S_A \, (E_a p = \emptyset_A (s, q)))$.

26. Intervention in Norm-Governed Worlds

In the examples of transmission of agency considered so far the operation of an automaton has been of type 'intervention in nature'. It should not be thought, however, that transmission of agency is confined to this category. This point is worth elaboration.

In the case of intervention in nature, the transition and output functions describe processes in nature. These are necessary at least in the sense of that which takes place independently of what agents do, a notion of necessity which was defined in (Df14).

In the case of the man who introduces metallic poison into a water container by the use of a lead pipe for the transportation of the water, the transition function maps the change of state which takes place when hydroxide is formed in the corrosion of lead that is exposed to air dissolved in water;

and the output function maps the dissolution of the poisonous hydroxide in water. The material details of these functions are not of any interest to us now, only their general character as functions mapping necessary processes in nature. Once the agent operating the automaton has intervened, nature takes over. That is to say, what happens *then* is necessary at least in the sense that it happens independently of agency and, *a fortiori*, independently of norm and prescription.

Compare intervention in nature with a case of 'intervention in a norm-governed world'. A person makes a declaration in which he directs the manner in which his assets shall be distributed after his death. The person is not under 21 years of age, nor of unsound mind, his declaration is written and signed at the end by him or by some other person at his direction and in his presence, the signature is made or acknowledged by the person in the presence of two witnesses, the witnesses are not totally blind or mentally deficient, and so forth. The case is familiar. We can think of all conditions, among these, which are not brought about by the person as constituting an internal state of an automaton without outputs. We can think of all the conditions that are brought about by the person as constituting an input of the automaton. And we can think of the next state as the existence of a valid will. If so, the transition function obviously describes what is the case when a valid norm is applied. The norm in question is a qualifying (constitutive) norm. It qualifies a declaration as a valid will and, hence, the maker of a declaration as a testator, on a complex (input and internal-state) condition. When this condition is fulfilled the norm is applicable. Applying the norm means attributing the quality of a valid will to the declaration, and it is this attribution that is specified by the transition function. Further, this attribution, clearly, is action done by norm-subjects — officials such as executors and judges. In short, the transition function describes what is the case when a valid norm is applied by norm-subjects; it describes what is the case when norm-subjects do what they are required to by a valid norm. Under this transition function a valid will exists, given the input and the internal state.

In this case, too, there is transmission of agency. A person who operates the automaton by making a declaration and thus supplying the input becomes a testator, i.e. the maker of a valid will. Further, when regarded from the point of view of the 'operator' the workings of the machine are just as much matters of necessity as are the natural processes in our previous examples. In either case we have processes which are necessary for the person operating the automaton, in the sense that they are independent of what he does; once he has supplied the input, nature or the application of norm by other persons takes over.

So there are obvious affinities between the two cases under consideration. But there is also one major difference. In the case of intervention in nature the functions of the automaton describe processes which are altogether independent of agency. In the case of intervention in a norm-governed world the functions describe processes which may be necessary for the intervening agent but which are certainly not processes in nature. On the contrary, they are strongly dependent on agency. The values of the functions are actions performed by norm-subjects. But, more importantly, for a fully developed case of a norm-governed world it seems essential that such actions be performed for reasons which include the circumstances that a valid norm is applicable. If this is correct, the transition function of an automaton representing a norm-governed world not only has actions as its values but the function itself is the outcome of actions done for certain reasons.

27. GRAMMARS

It has been shown how intervention in nature and intervention in a norm-governed world structure complex action. From now on we shall concentrate on the latter. And here the emphasis will be, not on the intervention as such, but on the general question of how norms must be organized if they are to generate action complexes that meet certain conditions, especially those that involve more than one agent. We shall use the theory of generative grammars as a general theoretical background, and we therefore begin the second half of the present chapter by indicating the nature of a generative grammar. (Salomaa (1973), is an excellent comprehensive survey of the theory of formal languages from the point of view of grammars. See also Luce *et al.* (1965, Part II)).

A grammar may be thought of as a set of norms or instructions for generating the members of a language. To illustrate this general conception we consider a semi-Thue system (STS). A STS consists of a finite set of *productions*, i.e. instructions as to how words over an alphabet may be transformed or manipulated. A production is given in the form $p \to q$ where p and q are words on the union of two disjoint, finite alphabets I_N and I_T of letters, called non-terminal and terminal letters, respectively. Such a production is said to be *applicable* to a word p' if and only if p' contains p as a subword, in which case there are (possibly empty) words p_1 and p_2 such that $p' = p_1 p p_2$. The *application* of an applicable production $p \to q$ to a word p' means replacing any subword p of p' by the word q for the reason that the production is applicable.

The operation of a STS consists of consecutive steps, each one of which involves one and only one application of a production. In the first step a fixed initial word is transformed. The sequence of steps may be stopped at any step, and the productions may be applied in any order.

Given a STS, the relation $p \Rightarrow q$ holds if and only if q may be generated or derived from p by exactly one application of a production $p' \rightarrow q'$. The relation $p \overset{*}{\Rightarrow} q$ holds if and only if $p = q$ or there is a finite *derivation (generation) sequence* $p = p_1 \Rightarrow p_2 \Rightarrow ... \Rightarrow p_n = q$ $(n \geqslant 2)$. $p \overset{*}{\Rightarrow} q$ clearly means that q can be got from p by zero or more applications of productions in the grammar concerned.

The language generated by a STS consists of all words over the terminal alphabet I_T which can be derived from the fixed initial word by means of the productions. So if p_0 is the initial word, the language generated by a STS is $\{p | p_0 \overset{*}{\Rightarrow} p\}$ where $p \in W(I_T)$.

More formally, a semi-Thue system is a construction $STS = (I_N, I_T, p_0, F)$ where I_N and I_T are disjoint, finite alphabets of non-terminal and terminal letters, $p_0 \in W(I_N \cup I_T)$ and F, the set of productions, is a class of pairs of words over $W(I_N \cup I_T)$, i.e. a binary relation over $W(I_N \cup I_T)$. It is customary to write (p, q) as $p \rightarrow q$ whenever $(p, q) \in F$.

The following construction is a STS:

$$(\phi, \{a, b\}, a, \{(a, bba)\})$$

It is immediately clear that the following is a generation sequence:

$a, bba, bbbba, bbbbbba.$

That is to say,

$a \Rightarrow bba \Rightarrow bbbba \Rightarrow bbbbbba$

all hold, relative to the grammar, and, hence, for example

$a \overset{*}{\Rightarrow} bbbba$

also holds. Further, each word in the sequence is a member of the language generated by this STS. This of course, is the set comprising the empty word and, in addition, all and only the words $b^{2n} a (n \geqslant 0)$.

The well-known Chomsky grammars may be defined by imposing restrictions on STS's. A STS is a Chomsky grammar provided that the initial word is a single non-terminal letter and no production is of the form $\lambda \rightarrow p$. The so-called Chomsky hierarchy is obtained by means of further restrictions on the productions of a Chomsky grammar and by means of proofs about the interrelations of the grammars so distinguished.

28. ORGANIZATIONS

When an alphabet is a repertoire a word over the alphabet is an action complex and a language over the alphabet a set of action complexes. A grammar for a set of action complexes defines an *organization* for this set.

Our main concern here is to form a conception of the nature of an organization. How should the components of a grammar be interpreted when the grammar is understood as an organization? What sort of a grammar should be used in this interpretation? We begin our consideration of these and related questions by indicating how a semi-Thue system $STS = (I_N, I_T, p_0, F)$ may be interpreted as an organization.

We let I_T be a repertoire. We let the members of I_N be relations other than act relations. We let the productions in F be given in the form $(p \supset \text{Shall } q)$ where the word p belongs to $W(I_N \cup I_T)$ and q is a word over the repertoire I_T. A production so defined is a norm that tells an agent how to proceed given a contingency. We may write $p \to q$ whenever $(p \supset \text{Shall } q)$ is a production and go on to define the relation $p \overset{*}{\Rightarrow} q$ in the usual way. The language generated by this 'semi-Thue organization' obviously is a set of activities. The following example illustrates the interpretation just outlined:

$$I_N = \{P_0\} \quad I_T = \{P_1, P_2, ..., P_6\}$$
$$F = \{f_1, f_2, ..., f_6\} \quad \text{where}$$

P_0 = the screws retaining plug-lid y are secured;
P_1 = x removes the screws retaining plug-lid y;
P_2 = x takes off plug-lid y;
P_3 = x pulls out the blown cartridge fuse from the contact clips;
P_4 = x inserts a new cartridge fuse;
P_5 = x replaces plug-lid y;
P_6 = x tightens the screws retaining plug-lid y;
f_i = $(P_{i-1} \supset \text{Shall } P_i)$ for $i = 1, 2, ..., 6$.

Each word in the language generated may be considered a one-element activity. Since each word therefore is a complex action, the grammar is an organization. In the operation of the organization, as in the operation of any STS, the norms are applied consecutively, one at a time. Since an activity is generated in each norm application, a sequence of norm applications, i.e. a derivation sequence, constitutes a proceeding. It is generally true that a derivation sequence in an organization not only generates an activity set but also structures this set temporally as a proceeding. The step structure of a derivation has here the same control role as the set of internal states in an automaton. We may say, therefore, that the operation of an organization generates both activities and proceedings.

In the particular case under consideration the total set of proceedings comprises the sequence $P_1 \Rightarrow P_2 \Rightarrow ... \Rightarrow P_6$ and, trivially, every subsequence. The first-mentioned is total in the sense that it orders the entire set of activities generated by the organization. We may call it 'replacing a blown cartridge fuse in a plug' and we can think of the organization as a grammar for this proceeding.

By definition, the structure of a proceeding generated by an organization is determined by the order in which norms are applied. If we want this order to be determined by the organization itself then it must somehow be built into the organization. There are several ways of doing this. For example, in a programmed organization the norms are labelled and the labels are used to specify which norms should be applied in the step following the application of a given norm. In other words, a norm in a programmed organization not only attaches a task to a condition but also specifies which norm or norms are to be applied next. The organization above may be considered a programmed organization since the application of a norm makes a unique norm applicable and hence determines which norm is to be applied in the next step of the operation of the organization. In an organization with a control set order is achieved in a different way: the sequence of norms corresponding to a derivation must belong to a set of such sequences specified in the definition of the organization. And still other ways of securing the structure of a proceeding are known. (For grammars with various control devices, see Salomaa (1973, Chapter V).)

There are variations on the interpretation theme outlined. It is for example not necessary that the members of the non-terminal alphabet be relations other than agent-causal relations, nor is it necessary that productions should always be norms of type obligation. We shall not stop to discuss such details, however. It is a matter of greater theoretical interest to realize that, though the interpretation of a grammar as an organization may be unproblematic in principle, the choice of grammar is not always as simple as our first example might suggest. In order to illustrate this we consider the following proceeding: a and b meet in the street, stop in front of each other, shake hands, exchange civil remarks and then say good-bye. What might a semi-Thue organization of this proceeding look like?

If we were prepared to regard groups of individuals as unitary agents and norm subjects, the answer would be clear immediately, for we would then be free to define a semi-Thue organization, or an organization of the Chomsky-type, in the usual way using collective agent-causal relations and norms addressed to the collective $\{a, b\}$ as subject. But we have already ruled out this solution on the ground that it conceals the problem of the structure of complex action. We must therefore seek to define the organization for the proceeding concerned in terms of instantiations of such predicates as

$$p_1(x, y) = x \text{ meets } y \text{ in the street}$$
$$p_2(x, y) = x \text{ stops in front of } y$$
$$p_3(x, y) = x \text{ shakes hands with } y$$
$$p_4(x, y) = x \text{ talks to } y \text{ about the weather, } y\text{'s job and family,}$$
$$\text{and } x \text{ refrains from being rude to } y$$
$$p_5(x, y) = x \text{ bids } y \text{ good-bye}$$

where the variable x is understood in the usual way as ranging over individual agents.

How, then, should the proceeding in question be defined? One possibility is to say that we have in fact got *two* proceedings in this case, the first of which is as follows: a meets b in the street, stops in front of him, shakes his hand, exchanges civil remarks with him and concludes the encounter by saying good-bye to him. The second proceeding present in the case is a synchronous, similar sequence of acts done by b with respect to a. If we understand the matter in this way, no problem is involved in defining organizations for the two individual proceedings. If care is taken over the temporal specifications, for conditions and tasks in the two cases, the temporal parallelism of the proceedings may be secured.

This solution seems adequate at least in respect of the prima-facie truth that there is simultaneous application of productions in the interaction or 'coaction' of a and b. But, on the other hand, the solution is at variance with the intuitively sound conception that we have in this case one proceeding — not two — resulting from the application of one and the same organization. The principle of the solution simply rules out the notion of a proceeding whose components are activities involving several agents or else it trivializes this notion by admitting *any* simultaneous proceedings of one-member activities as a proceeding of multi-member activities. It seems that, in order to be able to study the structure of complex action which we normally count as one proceeding and which involves the simultaneous contributions by two or more agents, we must use grammars of a different type as a model, *viz.* so-called developmental grammars or L-grammars, after Lindenmayer (1968, 1971) who was the first to introduce them in the abstract study of the cellular interactions of developing organisms. In the next section we shall discuss these and their interpretation as organizations.

29. L-GRAMMARS AND L-ORGANIZATIONS

An L-grammar is a word-manipulating system which differs from a normal grammar by virtue of the fact that all the letters of a word are rewritten in one step of the operation of the system. An L-system therefore permits the simultaneous application of several productions. A further distinguishing feature is that the language generated by an L-grammar is defined without reference to a divided alphabet, so if an L-grammar has a terminal and a non-terminal alphabet, this difference is not used to characterize the class of words generated by the grammar, although it may be used for other purposes. Lindenmayer motivated these novel features by reference to the intended application of L-systems in biology. He was concerned to study the stage-by-stage development of filamentous organisms. He interpreted each letter as the state of a cell and each word as the arrangement of states in an array of cells, i.e. as the stage of an organism in development. Accordingly the set of all words generated was considered the language generated by an L-grammar and the normal distinction between a terminal and a non-terminal alphabet could be dropped. Further, in order to capture the idea of simultaneous growth and development in an organism, it was necessary to stipulate that each letter of a word be rewritten in one step of the operation of the system in accordance with whatever instruction happens to be applicable.

Formally, an L-grammar is a construction $L = (I, p_0, F)$ where I is a non-empty alphabet, p_0, called the initial word, is a non-empty word over I, and F is a set of productions of the form $p \to q$, where p is a letter in and q is a word over I. In each step of the operation of the grammar an entire word is transformed by as many applications of productions to the word as there are letters in the word. This is reflected in the definition of the relation $\Rightarrow$ on $W(I)$. If p and q are words, then $p \Rightarrow q$ if and only if $p_1, p_2, ..., p_n$ are letters, $q_1, q_2, ..., q_n$ are words, $p = p_1 p_2 ... p_n$, $q = q_1 q_2 ... q_n$ $(n \geqslant 1)$ and there is for each i from 1 to n a production $p_i \to q_i$ in F. The relation $\overset{*}{\Rightarrow}$ is defined in the usual way as the reflexive, transitive closure of $\Rightarrow$ (cf. Section 27). Finally, the language generated by L is the set $\{p \mid p_0 \overset{*}{\Rightarrow} p\}$.

An L-grammar of this sort is, more precisely, an OL-grammar, i.e. an L-grammar with zero-sided input. This means that each production may be applied to a word in respect of a letter occurring in it independently of what the neighbouring letters are. So an OL-grammar is a context-free L-grammar. By contrast, in a L-grammar with one-sided input, called an 1L-grammar, the productions are given in the form $p^r \to q$ or $^r p \to q$, which means that the letter p may be replaced by the word q provided that its neighbour on the right (left) is r. And in a 2L-grammar, i.e. an L-grammar with two-sided input, the productions are given in the form ${}^r p^s \to q$.

Other variations are possible. An L-grammar is said to be deterministic if for each letter p there is exactly one word q such that $p \to q$ is a rule in F. An L-grammar is said to be propagating if there is no rule of the form $p \to \lambda$. To illustrate the general conception we give here an example of a propagating, deterministic L-grammar with zero-sided input:

$$(\{a, b\}, a, \{a \to b, b \to ab\})$$

This determines a unique derivation sequence, namely

$$a \Rightarrow b \Rightarrow ab \Rightarrow bab \Rightarrow abbab \Rightarrow bababbab \Rightarrow \ldots$$

which totally orders the words of the (infinite) language generated by the grammar.

For the interpretation of an L-grammar as an organization we assume, as before, that the alphabet is a repertoire. And we assume, secondly, that the productions are norms which instruct an agent how to proceed given that a condition is fulfilled. That is to say, if we disregard the possibility of the productions being permissive norms, we may assume that they are norms of the form $(p \supset \text{Shall } q)$ where p is a member of the repertoire and q is a proceeding of activities involving only one agent and, minimally, just one such activity, i.e. the performance of an action. For example, we might let I comprise the instantiations $p_i(a, b)$ and $p_i(b, a)$ $(i = 1, 2, 3, 4, 5)$ of the predicates listed in Section 28 above. The alphabet then defines a repertoire. If we next let F comprise the norms

(10)   (1) $(p_i(a, b) \supset \text{Shall } p_{i+1}(a, b))$ $i = 1, 2, 3, 4$
        (2) $(p_i(b, a) \supset \text{Shall } p_{i+1}(b, a))$

and let $p_1(a, b) \, p_1(b, a)$ be the initial word, we obtain an L-organization the operation of which results in the proceeding with two-member activities that we discussed in Section 28. The same proceeding but with a different internal structure results from the operation of the L-organization which is like the one just given except that F now comprises the norms

(11)   (1) $(p_i(a, b) \supset \text{Shall } p_{i+1}(b, a))$ $i = 1, 2, 3, 4$
        (2) $(p_i(b, a) \supset \text{Shall } p_{i+1}(a, b))$.

The difference between the two organizations, which is by no means immaterial, will be explored in Section 30 where we shall discuss it in terms of role structures.

Whether we use norms of the first or the second type, a further refinement of the structure of the proceeding may be introduced by treating the instant-tiations of $p_3(x, y)$ and $p_4(x, y)$, say, as descriptions of sub-proceedings, which result from the application of suitable productions in the organization. For the proceeding of shaking hands, for example, we might have norms which require x to shake y's hand at a time on the condition that he shook y's hand at the time immediately preceding that time (in the assumed discrete sequence of times). By specifying the time variable we can make sure that the organization provides for handshaking of suitable or standard length.

This simple example indicates that it is possible, using L-grammars, to obtain intuitively plausible structures for proceedings which two or more agents create and maintain. Just as in the original application of L-grammars in biology, organisms composed of independent cells with distinct boundaries were considered, so we consider groups of individual agents in the application outlined above. We describe the complex action of (in) a group by describing its progress or development, in discrete time steps, in terms of activities involving members of the group. The order of the component actions of an activity, in each step, reflects the array of the members involved. So instead of saying that we describe complex action in terms of multi-member activities we could also say, equivalently, that the description is given in terms of arrays of acting individuals. At each moment considered each agent in the array then prevailing applies a norm. In so doing he brings something about and acts for the reason of a condition which may have been brought about by himself or by some other agent. From the point of view of this analysis, an individual proceeding is a proceeding of one-member arrays, and a collective proceeding a proceeding of multi-member arrays. In connection with col-lective proceedings we may of course speak of 'collective actions' and 'col-lective agents', but this talk must then be understood exhaustively in terms of sets of individual agents and actions structured in a certain way.

30. ROLE STRUCTURES

In sociological theory the concept of a role is prominent as regards the detailed structuring of organizations. We therefore conclude this chapter by showing how the concept may be explicated within our theory.

In Section 26 we considered an example of a qualifying norm, *viz*. the norm which requires the attribution of the quality of being a testator to a person who fulfills certain conditions. Another example is the 'legal definition' which prescribes the attribution of the quality of being a young person to a person who has attained the age of fourteen years and is under the age of seventeen years. A third example is the norm which says that any person under the age of fourteen years is to be qualified as a child.

It is a characteristic feature of normally rich normative systems that they employ the attributes defined by such qualifying or constitutive norms as those in our three examples as conditions in norms of conduct. For instance, a normative system which has defined the attribute of being a child may go on to require that a child shall not take part in a performance or rehearsal the duration of which exceeds three and a half hours, that a child shall not take part in a performance or rehearsal if the duration of his appearances in the performance or rehearsal exceeds two and a half hours, that a child shall not be present at a place of performance or rehearsal before ten in the morning unless the child lives or receives education in that place, etc. If so, the normative system clearly uses an attribute defined in the system as the condition of some of its norms. Because of their prevalence in normative systems clusters of norms organized in this way deserve a name of their own. We shall call them role structures because in terms of them it is possible to define the sociological notion of a role.

More precisely, by a *role structure* we shall understand a set of at least two norms such that (i) all but one member of the set correlate positions with one and the same condition, and (ii) this condition appears as the position of the remaining member of the set. The norm referred to under (ii) is called the qualifying or constitutive norm of the role structure, and the norm or norms referred to under (i) are called its norms of conduct. By the position of a role structure we understand the position of its constitutive norm and by a role position we understand the position of some role structure. We say, finally, that the set of positions correlated in the norms of conduct of a role structure with its position constitutes a role. In the above example, 'child' denotes a role position, while not taking part in a performance or rehearsal the duration of which exceeds three and a half hours is an element of the associated role.

We now return to the organizations (10) and (11) defined in the previous section. Both may be broken up into role structures. For example, segment (1) of (10) comprises the following three role structures:

$$(12) \quad \begin{aligned} &(p_i(a, b) \supset \text{Shall } p_{i+1}(a, b)) \\ &(p_{i+1}(a, b) \supset \text{Shall } p_{i+2}(a, b)) \end{aligned} \qquad i = 1, 2, 3$$

And the role structures

$$(13) \quad \begin{aligned} &(p_i(a, b) \supset \text{Shall } p_{i+1}(b, a)) \\ &(p_{i+1}(b, a) \supset \text{Shall } p_{i+2}(a, b)) \end{aligned} \qquad i = 1, 2, 3$$

make up one half of (11). In either case the norms involved may be specified as, e.g., intentions or expectations. That the norms involved in the former case are thought of as intentions may be indicated thus:

$$
(14) \quad
\begin{aligned}
&B_a\,(p_i(a,\,b) \supset \text{Shall } p_{i+1}\,(a,\,b)) \\
&B_a\,(p_{i+1}\,(a,\,b) \supset \text{Shall } p_{i+2}\,(a,\,b))
\end{aligned}
\qquad i = 1, 2, 3
$$

That the same norms are conceived of as expectations means that

$$
(15) \quad
\begin{aligned}
&B_b\,(p_i(a,\,b) \supset \text{Shall } p_{i+1}\,(a,\,b)) \\
&B_b\,(p_{i+1}\,(a,\,b) \supset \text{Shall } p_{i+2}\,(a,\,b)).
\end{aligned}
\qquad i = 1, 2, 3
$$

The same procedure applied to the indicated half of (11) will give us

$$
(16) \quad
\begin{aligned}
&B_a\,(p_i(a,\,b) \supset \text{Shall } p_{i+1}\,(b,\,a)) \\
&B_a\,(p_{i+1}\,(b,\,a) \supset \text{Shall } p_{i+2}\,(a,\,b))
\end{aligned}
\qquad i = 1, 2, 3
$$

and

$$
(17) \quad
\begin{aligned}
&B_b\,(p_i(a,\,b) \supset \text{Shall } p_{i+1}\,(b,\,a)) \\
&B_b\,(p_{i+1}\,(b,\,a) \supset \text{Shall } p_{i+2}\,(a,\,b))
\end{aligned}
\qquad i = 1, 2, 3
$$

respectively. The role structures in (14) and (15) are pure whereas those in (16) and (17) are mixed. That is to say, in the former case the constituents of a role structure are of the same type — either intentions or expectations. In the latter cases the constituents are of different types. In each of the cases in (16) an expectation is the constitutive norm of the role structure while an intention is its norm of conduct; a here intends a role on the condition that b occupies a position defined by an expectation a has of b. In each of the cases in (17) the situation is reversed: b expects a to act in a role on the condition that b occupies a position defined in an intention of his. Role structures can obviously be mixed in a different way. For example, we might have a's intentions coupled with b's expectations, say the suitable pairs of members drawn from (14) and (15). Or we might have a's expectations coupled with b's expectations, for instance the suitable pairs of members drawn from (16) and (17).

Interlaced expectations and intentions are central in the social life of man; they constitute, almost literally, the fabric of social life. It is evident that when expectations are involved communication must intervene if the organizations to which they belong are to be applied and yield the proceedings they organize. The role of communication, primarily in the context of control, will be investigated in Chapter 5, which is devoted to social dynamics.

CHAPTER 4

CONTROL, INFLUENCE AND INTERACTION

In political science and sociology, especially social psychology, the concept of influence and the cognate notions of control and interaction occupy prominent positions. It is evident that they are all action concepts. It is therefore a task for the general theory of action to elucidate them. In what follows we attempt this task. We shall first concentrate on control in relation to an agent. There next follows an account of influence in relation to an agent, i.e. those interpersonal relations which determine the zone of control in relation to an agent. A subcategory of control and influence, called control and influence over an agent, is then distinguished, and in conclusion we show how the concepts explicated in the body of the chapter might be used to throw light on interaction.

31. CONTROL IN RELATION TO AN AGENT

Let $p(b)$ be a predicate which exhibits the singular term b (and possibly other singular terms). The act predicate $E_a p(b)$ then expresses an action by a *in relation to b with respect to b's being p*. For example, 'a brings it about that b is dead' expresses an action by a in relation to b with respect to the latter's death. We shall use the same jargon of predicates which are not of the form $E_a p(b)$ but which are equivalent, in the sense of (Df10), Section 9, to act predicates of this form. So in view of the fact that 'a kills b' is equivalent to 'a brings it about that b is dead', we say that the former expresses an action by a in relation to b with respect to b's being killed by a. In view of the fact that the same predicate is also equivalent to 'a brings it about that a kills b', we also say that it expresses an action by a in relation to a with respect to his killing b. Clearly, any act predicate expresses an action by an agent in relation to himself. Because of our emphasis on interpersonal influence we shall concentrate on action by an agent in relation to another (distinct) agent.

For the purposes of systematizing classes of actions in relation to an agent it is convenient to use the notion defined thus:

(Df19) Let p be a wff of L. (i) If p exhibits no operator $O \in Mo$, then the modal order (level) of p is 0 (zero). (ii) The modal order of p equals the highest of the modal orders of its components. (iii) If the modal order of p is n, then the modal order of Op is $n + 1$.

We shall also speak of the order or level of a modality and then mean the order or level of the wff which expresses the modality. In Section 19 we noted that valuations admit of level distinctions. The same is true of act predicates and relations. With reference to (5), Chapter 2, it may be said that there are exactly three action modalities of the nth order, for any agent a and any state of affairs p. In the special case when p in (5) is of the form $p(b)$ the three modalities concern a's action in relation to b. The joint assertion of (5) for $p_1(b), p_2(b), ..., p_m(b), m \geqslant 1$, yields a matrix of m^3 cells, which may be used for the description of a's action, of the nth order, in relation to b in m (independent) respects.

If the order of action modalities is not consistently maintained, the insistence that (5) be made the point of departure of the theory of normative positions is bound to seem arbitrary. For (iii) of (5) is ambiguous between the following two cases:

(iii') $E_a \sim (E_a p \vee E_a \sim p)$
(iv) $(\sim (E_a p \vee E_a \sim p) \mathbin{\&} \sim E_a \sim (E_a p \vee E_a \sim p))$.

So if we transgress a given order, there is no reason why (iii') should not replace (iii) in the initial classification of a space into mutually exclusive and collectively exhaustive possibilities. Since (iv) is ambiguous in the same way, there is no reason why we should not also add E_a(iv) as a possibility, and so on.

In the special case when p in (5) expresses an action with b as agent we shall call a's action in relation to b a *control* relation. That a walks on b's land is action by a in relation to b, but it is not of type control. On the other hand, if a brings it about that b walks on his land, the relation that a bears to b is a control relation.

There are 15 possible control relations that one agent can bear to another with respect to the latter's action with respect to one state of affairs. For let (5) be asserted for an agent b. This gives us three cases with respect to which, again according to (5), a can stand in one of three relations to b. Hence we must use a matrix of 3^3 cells for the specification of the control relations involved. Some of the cells turn out to be empty because the conditions $p_1(b), p_2(b)$, and $p_3(b)$ are not logically independent of one another. An inspection of the 27 cases will show that 15 are genuine possibilities. They may be listed in the following way:

(1.

	1	2	3	4	5	6	7	8	9	10	11	12	13	14	15)
$E_a E_b p$	+	+	+	+	–	–	–	–	–	–	–	–	–	–	–
$E_a \sim E_b p$	–	–	–	–	+	+	+	+	+	–	–	–	–	–	–
$E_a E_b \sim p$	–	–	–	–	+	+	–	–	–	+	+	–	–	–	–
$E_a \sim E_b \sim p$	+	+	–	–	–	–	+	–	–	–	–	+	+	–	–
$E_a \sim (E_b p \vee E_b \sim p)$	–	–	–	–	–	–	+	+	–	–	–	+	–	–	–
$E_a (E_b p \vee E_b \sim p)$	+	–	+	–	+	–	–	–	–	+	–	–	–	+	–

It is immediately seen that the description of a's control in relation to b in one or more respects requires the employment of act predicates of the $(n+1)$th level, if the description of those actions of b that are involved requires the use of act predicates of the nth level.

We shall distinguish between control and power relations. To specify the control relations from a to b in the way just described – by indicating what a does or does not do in relation to b with respect to b's actions – does not give much information about a's power in relation to b. To see this, consider for example

$$(1.14) \quad (\sim E_a E_b p \, \& \, \sim E_a \sim E_b p \, \& \, \sim E_a E_b \sim p \, \& \, \sim E_a \sim E_b \sim p \, \& \,$$
$$\sim E_a \sim (E_b p \vee E_b \sim p) \, \& \, E_a (E_b p \vee E_b \sim p)).$$

It is ambiguous in respect of its first conjunct, for this does not distinguish between the case where a can, but does not in fact, bring it about that b brings it about that p, and the case where a cannot, and therefore does not, bring it about that b brings it about that p. (1.14) is ambiguous in the same way in respect of several of its conjuncts, as a quick check of list (1) will make clear. In other words, (1.14) is compatible with different potential control relations from a to b in respect of p. It states a control relation, but leaves unspecified, or does not fully specify, the power which a has in relation to b. It is possible to distinguish between, on the one hand, action in relation to an agent and control as one of its subcategories and, on the other hand, social power and influence as one of its subcategories. So far only the first part of this distinction has received attention. We next turn to the second part.

32. ON THE POWER TO ACT

As we have already indicated, the influence a has in relation to b is specified by specifying what a *can* or *cannot* do in relation to b. In Section 6 we decided to use the modality M_a, defined in (Df6), for the purposes of referring to a's ability and opportunity to act. When 'can' is understood in this way there are exactly two cases to consider as regards a's power with respect to p, viz. $M_a E_a p$ and $\sim M_a E_a p$. The other two *prima facie* cases, $M_a \sim E_a p$ and $\sim M_a \sim E_a p$, must be ruled out. This is so because the latter is equivalent to $N_a E_a p$ and since N_a is an O*-necessity, it follows from the argument advanced in Section 25 that $\sim N_a E_a p$ or, equivalently, $M_a \sim E_a p$ is always true, for arbitrary agents a and arbitrary states of affairs p. For the purposes of specifying what a particular agent can or cannot do in a specific respect, $M_a \sim E_a p$ and $\sim M_a \sim E_a p$ are therefore quite unsuitable, the former because it is always true, the latter because it is never true. The suggested explication of 'can' shows that 'can' is always a 'can do'. In this respect the explication is intuitively sound.

For 'can do' in the context of the triadic action modality $E_a(p, q)$ we define

(Df20) Can $E_a(p, q) = \exists\, A\, \exists\, s \in S_A\, (q = \varnothing(s, p)\ \&\ M_a E_a p\ \&\ D_a s\ \&\ C'_a q)$.

The internal modalization of $E_a(p, q)$ which is used as definiens in (Df20) comes closer than the external modalization $M_a E_a(p, q)$ to the assertion that it is within a's power to bring about q by bringing p about, for it says that there exists an automaton which a can operate, in respect of the input element p. (This point was made in discussion by Professor Stig Kanger.) If we allow ourselves to quantify over conditions, including propositions, we can bind the first variable of Can $E_a(p, q)$ and introduce the definition

(Df21)   Can $E_a p = \exists\, q$ Can $E_a(q, p)$

according to which Can $E_a p$ means that it is within a's power to bring p about by some measure or other. According to (Df20) and (Df21) neither Can$\sim E_a p$ nor $\sim$Can$\sim E_a p$ are well-defined. $M_a p$ is equivalent to $(C_a p \vee C'_a \sim p)$. It is therefore plain that $E_a p$ implies $M_a E_a p$ and, in view of (3), Chapter 3, it may thus be seen that $E_a p$ implies Can $E_a p$ and, conversely, that $\sim$Can $E_a p$ implies $\sim E_a p$.

33. INFLUENCE AND SOCIAL POWER

It follows from the previous section that a's power to act in relation to b with respect to just one condition can be of only two types. We may also express this by saying that in the *scope* $\{p(b)\}$, a's power can be of the type Can $E_a p(b)$ or of the type $\sim$Can $E_a p(b)$. Similarly, in the scope $\{p(b)$, $q(b)\}$ a's power can be of four types:

$(Can\ E_a p(b)\ \&\ Can\ E_a q(b))$

$(Can\ E_a p(b)\ \&\ \sim Can\ E_a q(b))$

$(\sim Can\ E_a p(b)\ \&\ Can\ E_a q(b))$

$(\sim Can\ E_a p(b)\ \&\ \sim Can\ E_a q(b))$.

Generally speaking, in a scope of length n the power of an agent can be of 2^n types.

An agent's power to act in relation to another agent falls in the category of *social power*. An agent's power in a scope of control relations is termed his *influence* in this scope. Influence so understood is of course a subcategory of social power. (This notion of influence differs from that investigated in Pörn (1970, Chapter 2). The latter is a subcategory of control as defined in Section 31. We now reserve the term 'influence' for a subcategory of social power because there appears to be a tendency in this direction in sociology and political science.) In Section 35 we shall further distinguish a subcategory of control, called control 'over' an agent, together with its potential counterpart, influence 'over' an agent.

For the purposes of mapping classes of influence relations it may be useful to distinguish between orders or levels of influence. This distinction is easily illustrated. Let b's control in relation to c, e.g. $Can\ E_b p(c)$, be of the nth order. We may then define control of the $(n+1)$th order since the presence or absence of b's control in relation to c may be the result of a's action, as in the case $E_a\ Can\ E_b p(c)$: a makes it possible for b to act in relation to c. The power of a to act in this way is clearly of the $(n+1)$th order and expressed by $Can\ E_a\ Can\ E_b p(c)$. The ability to prevent an agent from taking action in relation to an agent is similarly influence of a higher order, in the present example expressed by $Can\ E_a \sim Can\ E_b p(c)$.

34. ON THE MEASUREMENT OF INFLUENCE

This is a topic which has been widely discussed in the social sciences. We shall not try to develop it here in any great detail. Instead we choose to work out an example illustrating an approach to measurement of influence which in some contexts is natural and, from the point of view of our conception of influence, readily applicable.

Consider a committee $C = \{b_1, b_2, b_3, b_4\}$ such that b_1 and b_2 has one vote each, b_3 has two votes, and b_4 three votes. We assume it takes five votes to carry a measure, i.e. the members of any coalition must between them have at least five votes if the coalition is to win. It has long been recognized that the number of votes a member of a voting body has is not in itself a good measure of his power. For example, in the case of our C it cannot happily be asserted that b_4 has three times as much power as b_1, for in the event that b_4 can influence b_3 to support him on a measure, b_4 is a virtual dictator and b_1 is powerless.

A more successful power index is that developed by L. S. Shapley and M. Shubik. (See Shapley and Shubik (1954), and also Kemeny, *et al.* (1964, pp. 108–110) for the example discussed below.) This index relates to the number of ordered coalitions of which a committee member is the determining member or *pivot*. The members of the committee are ordered according to how likely they are to vote for a measure; call this arrangement an alignment. If the first m members of an alignment is a winning coalition with but is not a winning coalition without the mth member, then this member is said to be the pivot of the alignment in question. The frequency with which a given committee member is the pivot in an alignment constitutes the Shapley-Shubik measure of his power, if the frequency is taken over the class of all possible alignments.

In our example there are 4! alignments. They are shown in Table IV.

TABLE IV

Possible alignments in a 4-member committee

$b_1 b_2 b_3 b_4$	$b_2 b_1 b_3 b_4$	$b_3 b_2 b_1 b_4$	$b_4 b_2 b_3 b_1$
$b_1 b_2 b_4 b_3$	$b_2 b_1 b_4 b_3$	$b_3 b_2 b_4 b_1$	$b_4 b_2 b_1 b_3$
$b_1 b_3 b_2 b_4$	$b_2 b_3 b_1 b_4$	$b_3 b_1 b_2 b_4$	$b_4 b_3 b_2 b_1$
$b_1 b_3 b_4 b_2$	$b_2 b_3 b_4 b_1$	$b_3 b_1 b_4 b_2$	$b_4 b_3 b_1 b_2$
$b_1 b_4 b_2 b_3$	$b_2 b_4 b_1 b_3$	$b_3 b_4 b_2 b_1$	$b_4 b_1 b_2 b_3$
$b_1 b_4 b_3 b_2$	$b_2 b_4 b_3 b_1$	$b_3 b_4 b_1 b_2$	$b_4 b_1 b_3 b_2$

In each alignment the pivot is italicized. We see that b_1 and b_2 are pivotal twice, b_3 six times, and b_4 fourteen times. That is to say, they have $1/12$, $1/12$, $3/12$, and $7/12$ power, respectively. This is the *a priori voting strength* in our committee C. Let $\Pi_i(C)$ be the *a priori* voting strength of b_i in C.

Suppose next that we have empirically determined the influence of an agent a in the scope $\{p(b_i)\}$, where $i = 1, 2, 3, 4$ and $p(b_i)$ is b_i's action of voting for the measure concerned. If Can $E_a p(b_i)$, we let a's influence in relation to b_i with respect to the measure equal $\Pi_i(C)$; if ~Can $E_a p(b_i)$, a's influence in relation to b_i is zero. By taking the sum of these measures of a's influence we obtain the measure of a's influence in the scope $\{p(b_i)\}$. For example, if

$$\sim\!\text{Can } E_a p(b_1)$$
$$\text{Can } E_a p(b_2)$$
$$\text{Can } E_a p(b_3)$$
$$\sim\!\text{Can } E_a p(b_4)$$

a's influence in the scope $\{p(b_i)\}$ is 4/12 or, simplified, 1/3. It is of course possible that $a = b_i$ for some i from 1 to 4. In this case we need not assume that Can $E_{b_i} p(b_i)$. The two measures are and should be kept distinct. The *a priori* voting strength of a member concerns his position in a structure defined by certain rules. The strength of a member's influence, on the other hand, inheres in factors external to that structure. It may therefore be *less* than his *a priori* voting strength, e.g. a member with the right to vote in a committee may not be able to exercise this right for reasons which have nothing to do with his structural position in the committee.

It is plain that the suggested measure of influence is forthcoming only in cases which are sufficiently well-structured to make the determination of *a priori* strength possible.

35. CONTROL OVER AN AGENT

It is possible to distinguish a subcategory of control which it seems appropriate to call control *over* an agent (in some respect or other). Suppose that a locks b in a room and thereby brings it about that b does not keep an appointment. It is then true that a stands in a control relation to b with respect to b's not keeping the appointment. Now compare this control relation with that which obtains when a persuades b not to keep, or deters b from keeping, the appointment. The latter, unlike the former, necessarily involves an 'intentional channel', i.e. b, the persuaded agent, grounds this action on an intention brought about by the persuading agent a. In the former case nothing of this sort need be involved: in walking into the room b might well have applied an intention the formation of which was completely independent of a's action.

The construction $E_a \sim\! E_b p$, 'a brings it about that b does not keep the appointment', is not sufficient to bring out the difference between the two cases. For this purpose we must use the three-place action modality $E_a(p, q)$ defined in (Df17). The structure of the first case is given by $E_a(p(a, b), \sim\! E_b p)$, where $p(a, b)$ is to the effect that a locks b in a room. The structure of the second case is given by $E_a(B_b \text{ Shall } \sim\! E_b p, \sim\! E_b p)$, where we have in the antecedent an explicit mention of b's intention not to keep the appointment. It is this intentional element which is required for control over an agent.

To elucidate further the nature of control over an agent we consider

(2) $E_a(B_b \text{ Shall } E_b q, E_b q)$.

By (Df17), this is the statement

(3) $\exists A \exists s \in S_A (E_b q = \emptyset_A (s, B_b \text{ Shall } E_b q) \, \& \, E_a B_b \text{ Shall } E_b q \, \& $
$D_a s \, \& \, C_a' E_b q)$

In view of our discussion in Chapter 2, it is not now hard to see how the internal state s of the automaton concerned should be specified: s is the state b is in when he brings q about intentionally, i.e. s is the state described by

(4) $E_b(B_b \text{ Shall } E_b q \supset E_b q)$.

Thus, if P. M. Wilson persuades Mr. Smith to vote Labour, the following conditions are all fulfilled: (i) Wilson brings it about that Smith intends to vote Labour; (ii) it is necessary for something Wilson does that Smith executes his intention to vote Labour; and (iii) but for Wilson's action Smith might not vote Labour.

According to the suggested analysis of control over an agent, the action of convincing an agent – causing him to believe something – is always involved in a case of such control. This action may itself be done by performing some other action; for example, one may persuade an agent to take action by doing some action or other. This action often takes the form of giving the agent a reason for action. Thus, the statement that Wilson persuades Smith to vote Labour by convincing Smith that he is not going to try to control inflation should be understood as having the form

(5) $(E_a(B_b p, B_b \text{ Shall } E_b q) \, \& \, E_a(B_b \text{ Shall } E_b q, E_b q))$.

The first conjunct, which says that a gives b a reason for action is equivalent to

(6) $\exists A \exists s \in S_A (B_b \text{ Shall } E_b q = \emptyset_A (s, B_b p) \, \& \, E_a B_b p \, \& \, D_a s \, \& $
$C_a' B_b \text{ Shall } E_b q)$.

The internal state s of the automaton concerned is the state expressed by

(7) $B_b(p \supset \text{ Shall } E_b q)$

i.e. the state b is in when he intends to bring q about on the condition that p. Accordingly, if the statement mentioned above is true, we must add the following conditions to (i)–(iii): (iv) Wilson convinces Smith that he is not going to try to control inflation; (v) it is necessary for something Wilson does that Smith intends to vote Labour on the condition that Wilson is not going to try to control inflation.

Exercising suasion over an agent by giving him a reason for action may be
termed activation of commitment. This case may be contrasted with that
in which suasion is achieved by inducing a commitment in an agent. The place
of (5)–(7) is then taken by

(8) $(E_a(B_b(p \supset \text{Shall } E_b q), B_b \text{ Shall } E_b q) \& E_a(B_b \text{ Shall } E_b q, E_b q))$

(9) $\exists A \exists s \in S_A (B_b \text{ Shall } E_b q = \emptyset_A (s, B_b(p \supset \text{Shall } E_b q)) \&$

$E_a B_b(p \supset \text{Shall } E_b q) \& D_a s \& C_a' B_b \text{ Shall } E_b q)$

(10) $B_b p$

respectively. Control over an agent, of the kind described by (2), is present
in both cases, as is evident from (5) and (8). The two cases differ with respect
to the way in which the action of convincing an agent is accomplished. In
activation of commitment a convinces b that an intention b has, perhaps
independently of what a does or has done, is applicable, whereas in a case
of inducing a commitment a brings it about that b has an intention which is
applicable in virtue of beliefs which b has and, perhaps, has independently of
what a does or has done.

To avoid misunderstanding it should be stressed that suasion may be
complex in such a way that both activation and inducement of commitment
are exemplified in it. But this circumstance does not necessitate the introduction of any additional analytical categories. If, for example, a case of complex
suasion is a proceeding, then the present categories suffice, for we may then
describe the structure of the case by treating the result of activation and
inducement of commitment as a sequential input of an automaton of a
suitable sort.

The cases of control over an agent considered so far are all special cases.
It may be said, quite generally, that control over an agent may be characterized by means of statements of the form

(11) $E_a(p(b), q(b))$

and general logical means such as connectives. In (11) $p(b)$ expresses an
intention of b which may be more or less complex in the same way as
normative positions or tasks may be more or less complex; $q(b)$ expresses the
corresponding 'correct' action, i.e. the action b does if and only if b applies
his intention, which, it should be stressed, is not to say that $q(b)$ expresses
that b applies the intention expressed by $p(b)$.

We have suggested that control over an agent may be subdivided into activation and inducement of commitment. It is possible further to distinguish,

in either case, between positive and negative control, or between suasion and coercion (deterrence). Coercion is conceptually connected with the action of depriving an agent of things he strongly wants to retain, suasion with the action of supplying an agent with things he wants to obtain. The distinction between them thus concerns the character of the wants that surround the intention which we have said is characteristically involved in control over an agent.

Influence over an agent requires now no special treatment. It is of course a subcategory of influence in relation to an agent, that subcategory in which an agent's power to act in relation to another is confined to control over him.

36. ON COMMUNICATION AND CONTROL

In the previous section we made the act of convincing an agent a component of control over him. We made no reference to communication, and this may seem surprising in view of the fact that control, especially control over an agent, is frequently linked with communication. The joint investigation of the two notions is a task of some magnitude. In Chapter 5 we shall study certain aspects of the topic in some detail. Here we shall give only the bare minimum required for a perspective on our conception of control. We use constructions of both the form $E_a B_b p$ and the form $E_a(p, B_b q)$, where p may but need not be of the form $B_b r$, to describe cases of the kind that interest us. First we introduce some auxiliary notions.

We shall say that an agent is informed that p, or that he has the information that p, if and only if he truly believes that p. Convincing him that p need not amount to informing him that p for the simple reason that the belief he is caused to acquire need not be true.

We shall also say that an agent takes p to be a sufficient reason for believing that q if and only if he believes that $(p \supset q)$. That he believes that q for the reason that p thus means that he believes that p and takes p to be a sufficient reason for believing that q (cf. Section 16). This is different from his being informed that q for the reason that p, which in turn is different from his being informed that q for the reason that he is informed that p, and so on.

Assume now that

(12) $(E_a B_b p \ \& \ D_a B_b (p \supset q) \ \& \ C'_a B_b q)$

is true. The assumption means that a convinces b that q by giving him a reason for believing that q, and it entails that a convinces b that q by convincing him that p since (12) implies $E_a(B_b p, B_b q)$. By contrast, if

$$(13) \quad (E_a B_b (p \supset q) \,\&\, D_a B_b p \,\&\, C'_a B_b q)$$

is true, a convinces b that q by making him take p as a sufficient reason for believing that q.

(12) is of crucial importance to our next task, which is to describe *indication* and *signalling action*. To this end we consider an organization comprising expectations which an agent a has vis-à-vis another agent b. Thus, for a number of conditions p and q we have

$$(14) \quad B_a (p \supset \text{Shall } E_b q).$$

For example, a's expectations might be that b should hoist Flag 1 if he is on speed trials, Flag 2 if he is disabled, Flag 3 if he needs assistance, and so on. In the context of (14) a situation such that

$$(15) \quad B_a (\text{Shall } E_b q \supset E_b q)$$

and

$$(16) \quad B_a (E_b q \supset p)$$

are both true is now highly significant. (15) says that a believes that b carries out his tasks, while (16) says that a takes b's bringing q about as a sufficient reason for believing that p. Against the background of (14) the conjunction of (15) and (16) says that a believes that b's execution of a task fulfils an expectation he has vis-à-vis b. The conjunction of (14)–(16) or its logical equivalent, *viz.*

$$(17) \quad B_a ((p \supset \text{Shall } E_b q) \,\&\, (\text{Shall } E_b q \supset E_b q) \,\&\, (E_b q \supset p)),$$

may be embedded in structures of type (12) in the following way:

$$(18) \quad (E_b B_a E_b q \,\&\, D_b (17) \,\&\, C'_b B_a p)$$

This implies

$$(19) \quad (E_b B_a E_b q \,\&\, D_b (16) \,\&\, C'_b B_a p)$$

which says that b convinces a that p by giving a a reason for believing that p, namely that he (b) brings q about. In the more comprehensive structure (18) this act of convincing a is normatively mediated because a's belief that b fulfils his expectation is there necessary for something he does.

In case (18) we shall say that b *indicates* that p to a by convincing him that he brings it about that q. In other words, we take indication to be an act of convincing an agent which is normatively mediated in the sense outlined. Measures which are not themselves acts of convincing an agent and by means of which indication is achieved will be called *signals* or *signalling actions*.

In case (18) b's indication to a that p is done by convincing a that b brings
it about that q. This act is *not* a signal, but if it is done by means of an act
which is not itself an act of convincing, the latter is a signal, and, as we may
say without risk of confusion, a signal to a that p. So if, to return to our
example, b indicates to a that he is on speed trials by convincing him that he
hoists Flag 1, and if he does the latter by hoisting Flag 1, which is easily done
if a is in a good position to observe what b does, then b's hoist is indeed a
signalling action and, more precisely, a signal to a that he is on speed trials.
In this case the signal actually made is the same as the signal prescribed in a's
expectation. However, such an identity is no necessity. If b indicates to a
that he is on speed trials by hoisting Flag 2, b's hoist is a signal to a that he
is on speed trials, but the signal actually made is not the signal prescribed.

The case we have described may be thought of as an instance of the operation of a signalling system. The system is defined as the organization which
comprises

$$(20) \qquad B_a(p_i \supset \text{Shall } E_b q_i)$$

for a number i ($i = 1, 2, ..., n$) of conditions p_i and hoists q_i. (18) when
asserted for some i from 1 to n, describes an instance of the operation of the
system, and a statement $E_b(r, B_a E_b q)$ says that b operates the system by
making the signal r.

It follows immediately from our account that the indication of a state of
affairs to an agent need not amount to informing him that the state obtains.
The information conveyed by the system (20) may therefore be more or less
complete over the range $\{p_i\}$. We shall use the term 'communication' as a
general label to refer to all cases of convincing somebody that something is
the case. Indicating, with or without signalling, and informing are thus subcategories of communication. In this vein we shall call the agent who is in the
position of b in our example a communicator, and the agent who is in the
position of a in our example an audience.

Other consequences follow. For example, a communicator who, say,
indicates a state of affairs need not mean or intend to do so; if he does intend
to indicate the state of affairs, he may or may not succeed; he may indicate
his intention without intending to do so; and if he does intend to indicate
his intention he may or may not succeed. Similarly, a communicator who
indicates a state of affairs need not be informed that that is what he does, nor,
if he does it by signalling, need he have the information that he makes a
signal. Finally, though the norms making up a signalling system need not be
previously agreed, it is pretty plain, first, that the operation of a signalling
system, if it is to be at all reliable from the point of view of the audience,

requires such an agreement and, secondly, that the agreement, if it is to be made, requires that the audience inform the communicator of his expectations. The relevance of this last remark may be clearly seen in the case of role structures exhibiting expectations, such as those described in (15)–(17) in Chapter 3. If the organizations of which these structures are constituents are to yield the proceedings they organize, the expectations must be communicated and the communicator's signalling action made in some reliable manner. In fact, a comparatively complex sequence of transmission of agency must be present. For illustration, consider the expectation of the role structures (17). A typical sequence of the kind indicated might be as follows:

The communicator b informs the audience a of his expectations and, hence,

(21) $E_b(q, B_a B_b (p_{i+1}(b, a) \supset \text{Shall } p_{i+2}(a, b)))$

is true for some action q; by making a receive his expectations b induces the corresponding commitments, i.e.

(22) $E_b(B_a B_b (p_{i+1}(b, a) \supset \text{Shall } p_{i+2}(a, b)), B_a(p_{i+1}(b, a) \supset \text{Shall } p_{i+2}(a, b)))$;

the inducement of commitments is here coupled with convincing as in

(23) $E_b(B_a(p_{i+1}(b, a) \supset \text{Shall } p_{i+2}(a, b)), B_a \text{ Shall } p_{i+2}(a, b))$;

finally, the act of convincing is part of control, or

(24) $E_b(B_a \text{ Shall } p_{i+2}(a, b), p_{i+2}(a, b))$.

Because the transmission relation described by our three-place action modality is transitive, (21)–(24) have a number of implications. In particular, they imply

(25) $E_b(q, p_{i+2}(a, b))$

That is to say, by performing an action which is in fact a signalling action b makes a do the things he expects him to do. Communication is here essential to the exercise of control over an agent.

37. ACTION IN CONSEQUENCE RELATIONS

In Section 31 the notion of an action in relation to an agent was defined. This notion is very general indeed; it includes, for example, communication, for, clearly, a acts in relation to b if a convinces b of something. Though general, the notion admits a generalization. Following the pattern set in

Section 31 we might say that a predicate $F_a p(b)$ expresses an action by a in *consequence* relation to b (with respect to b's being p) and thus obtain a generalization of the notion of an action in relation to an agent. That this is a genuine generalization is evident from the fact that the following, but not its converse, is logically true:

(26) $(E_a p \supset F_a p)$.

If the suggested generalization is accepted, several of the notions introduced in this chapter receive a corresponding generalization. For example, in the special case where $p(b)$ expresses an action with b as agent we would speak of a's control in consequence relation to b whenever $F_a p(b)$ is true. This category has control in relation to an agent, defined in Section 31, as a subcategory. We similarly obtain a generalized notion of control over an agent by replacing E_a in (11) by F_a as defined in (Df18), Section 24. And we get of course a generalized notion of communication.

For an illustration, consider

(27) $(E_a B_b p \ \& \ B_b (p \supset q) \ \& \ C'_a B_b q)$

got from (12) by weakening the second conjunct. (27) implies

(28) $F_a (B_b p, B_b q)$

but not the stronger formula $E_a (B_a p, B_b q)$. Now, there is nothing far-fetched about a situation of the kind described by (27); for example, a convinces b that c is a liar, independently of what a does b believes that if c is a liar, he will not keep the business secret he told him some time ago, and but for a's action b might not believe that c will not keep the secret. In view of the fact that (27) logically implies (28), it is also true of this situation that it follows from the fact that a convinces b that c is a liar that b believes that c will not keep the secret. Other examples of such weak counterfactual dependence between actions of different agents are easily constructed. It would therefore, it seems, be dogmatic to exclude actions in consequence relations to an agent from considerations pertaining to social action or interaction.

38. INTERACTION

One form of interaction may be defined in terms of action in relation to an agent: two agents interact if they act in relation to each other. This form may be further structured by means of notions now available to us. So far, in the present chapter, we have defined three classes of action complexes within the category of actions in relation to an agent. Representing the classes by closed curves we have the relations of inclusion shown in the following figure:

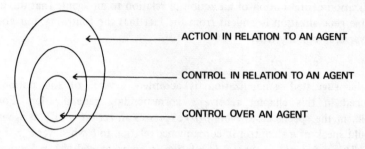

Fig. 2.   Inclusions among actions in relation to an agent.

We see immediately from the figure that we can define three types of action complexes: (1) action in relation to an agent which is not also control in relation to him; (2) control in relation to an agent which is not also control over him; and (3) control over an agent. These types may be used to subdivide the form of interaction under consideration into three varieties. The interaction between *a* and *b* is of the first type if *a* walks on *b*'s land and *b* walks on *a*'s land, or if *a* kills *b* and *b* kills *a*. It is of the second type if, for example, *a* prevents *b* from keeping an appointment and *b* prevents *a* from repaying a debt. And it is of the third type if, for example, *a* persuades *b* to vote Labour and *b* persuades *a* not to vote.

By making use of the notion introduced in the previous section we may obtain a more general notion of interaction: two agents interact if they act in consequence relations to each other. Is the condition which is here sufficient for interaction also necessary? We consider the following example: *a* intends to assist his wife *b* on the condition that she is seriously ill; he is now convinced of *b*'s illness and derives the intention to cancel an appointment with *c*; and he executes the derived intention. According to our account in Section 17 it is then the case that *a* cancels the appointment with *c* with the intention of assisting *b*. It is also true that *a* acts in relation to *c*, but on the assumption that *a* has derived rather than evolved his intention to cancel the appointment from his intention to assist *b*, it is *not* true that *a* acts in relation to *b*. Let us say, for short, that *a refers* his action to *b* (or *b*'s illness) when his action in relation to *b* is in this way 'intentionally contained' in his action in relation to *c*. It would be entirely in line with usage in sociology to define a form of interaction thus: two agents interact if they refer their actions to each other. We shall do this and accept the following general characterization: two agents interact if and only if they act in consequence relation to each other or refer their actions to each other. It is evident that the two forms of interaction are mutually independent; it is possible for an agent to act in relation to another without referring his action to him and, conversely, it is possible for an agent to refer an action to an agent without acting in relation to him. The two forms of interaction are therefore useful dimensions for the description of action complexes.

39. SOCIAL GROUPS AND SOCIAL SYSTEMS

Let S be an aggregation of agents. A subset C of S of not less than three members is said to form a *clique* or *social group* in S provided, first, that any two members of C habitually or recurrently interact with each other and, secondly, that C is not a proper subset of members of S with the first property. In other words, a social group in an aggregation is a maximal sub-group of at least three members, each of whom interacts with every other member. (Compare Chapple and Coon) (1941, pp. 281–287), Luce (1950) and Homans (1951, Chapter 4).)

S may not contain any social groups. If it does contain social groups, a member of S is non-cliqual if he does not belong to any cliques, uni-cliqual if he belongs to exactly one clique, and so forth. (For these and kindred notions, see Harary (1959).)

Let S be the set $\{a_1, a_2, ..., a_9\}$. Let the interaction pattern in S be as represented in Figure 3. The diagram gives only the matrix of interaction symmetries in S. It may be seen from inspection of the diagram that there are five social groups in S: $C_1 = \{a_1, a_2, a_3\}$, $C_2 = \{a_3, a_5, a_6, a_7\}$, $C_3 = \{a_3, a_4, a_5, a_7\}$, ..., that $\{a_7, a_8, a_9\}$ is not a social group in S, and so forth. But in

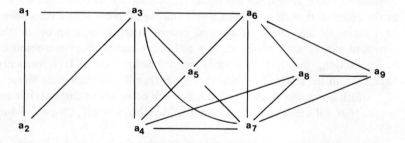

Fig. 3.   Interaction pattern in an aggregation of agents.

other respects the representation does not reveal much. It says nothing about the interaction frequencies and therefore nothing about the distance between the members of S, it leaves unspecified the forms of interaction involved in each pair, and it does not make clear in what respects the interacting pairs interact. For a more precise definition of the social groups in S all of these aspects and factors must be specified. For example, in the more precise definition of C_1 we might have the specification that a_1 and a_2 interact as, respectively, seller and buyer of food, that a_1 and a_3 interact in the same way, that a_2 interacts with a_1 more frequently than a_3, that a_2 and a_3 interact as spouses in such-and-such a scope of activities, etc.

The interactions that define a social group may be the results of applying different organizations. We shall therefore distinguish between social groups and social systems. A *social system* is a social group in union with an organization and a power structure. The organization supplies the norms for the members of the group, while the power structure determines what agents can or cannot do in relation to each other. The interactions of the organization and the power structure constitute an important aspect of a social system.

A community may be understood as a network of social systems. If our sample aggregation S is the population of a miniature community, the community comprises five social systems. It is evident, from the example alone, that the detailed analysis of communities quickly becomes a matter of great complexity. For example, to see why a_2 and a_4 are not cocliqual, or why the distance between C_2 and C_3 is less than the distance between C_1 and C_2, it may be necessary to supply details of the community structure the complexity of which is already quite impressive.

By a *social order* we understood the order of actions in a community. The social order arises as the joint product of the actions of the community members. However, as these are in the first instance members of this or that constituent social system, an individual is governed by its norms and subject to the constraints of its power structure. The overall order need not therefore be known by any member, nor, of course, need its production be the conscious aim of any individual. A social order comes about as a result of human action, but not necessarily with human design. It is certainly important, in the study of social orders, to distinguish between those features of it which come about with, and those which come about without, human design. (For a discussion of this distinction, see Hayek (1967, Chapters 4 and 6).)

We conclude this chapter with some remarks on the basis of social order.

40. The basis of social order

Let us consider a human individual in some environment. According to our dominant conception he is an agent, a being capable of initiating action and as such a source of activity. He is also a reacting creature. As such he reacts or responds to changes in his environment in accordance with the demands made of it by his desires.

We think that two high-level axioms or postulates may be used to characterize the human individual as an acting and reacting being and, by implication, to throw light on the basis of social order. These are the axiom of rationality and the axiom of free will. (For a discussion of these and how they may be used to solve the Prisoner's Dilemma, see Howard (1966a), and Sections 47 and 48 below.) The first is well-known in the theory of games (interdependent decision). It says that of two alternative actions which give rise to outcome a rational agent chooses the action which yields the outcome that is more wanted by him provided that he believes that he can do the action, and that the outcome will be realized if he does the action and will not be realized if he does the alternative action.

Rationality of this kind presupposes knowledge or belief in the form of predictions of the kind: if action p is done in circumstances C, then outcome q will be realized. When the action has the character of being an interference in the physical environment, knowledge of the kind required for exercise of rationality is knowledge of the order in nature. This order is invariable and inherent in 'the nature of things', i.e. derives from the stable properties of objects. Because of its invariability it is relatively easy to predict. The well-grounded predictions man uses to transmit his agency to attain the ends set by his intentions and ultimately, according to our principle of ideality (stated in Section 18), by his wants.

By comparison, the social environment of the human individual is not an inherently orderly environment. (This is argued persuasively in Kelvin (1969, Chapter 1).) As a result his ability to make reliable predictions is much more limited. In the social environment he encounters other agents, or decision-makers. Between them these share a repertoire which is very large indeed. However, it is not the size of the repertoire which limits man's ability to predict. The limitations are contingent on the open-ended character of the human will, or this at any rate is what the axiom of free will asserts. It asserts that if one agent predicts how another agent will act, the latter has a choice whether or not to act in accordance with the prediction, and it asserts this for absolutely all predictions that any agent can make vis-à-vis the actions of another agent, including predictions made on the basis of the axiom of

rationality. (It must be understood here that the prediction is made by selecting one possibility from an agent's choice-state, i.e. the set of action possibilities
open to the agent in a given situation.)

Why, then, does not the social environment become altogether un-
predictable? If the will is free in the sense intended by the axiom of free will,
why are there social orders? The answer, it seems, must be spelt out by
reference to the axiom of rationality. The exercise of rationality demands,
as we have already said, that man acquire knowledge of events that are
contingent on others so that he can predict the former on the basis of his
knowledge of the latter. The unconstrained operation of the will threatens
predictability and, hence, it is incompatible with rational action. Since no
constraints are inherent in the will, as its invariable features, it is practically
necessary to impose or create constraints in order to secure predictability.
This is done through actions of type prescription and through actions of
other type, prevention for example. Unable to find uniform regularities in
the world of agency, to match his discovery of invariable laws of nature, man
makes and maintains regularities to secure the predictability which rational
action requires. This is what Nietzsche meant when he characterized the herd's
morality of truthfulness by saying that its central demand is: 'You shall be
knowable, express your inner nature by clear and constant signs — otherwise
you are dangerous' (from Section 277 of Nietzsche (1968).)

Apart from elaborations, and some long and complex elaborations are
possible here, this is what our claim amounts to: the bases of social order may
be understood in terms of the union of two axioms, the axiom of rationality
and the axiom of free will.

CHAPTER 5

SOCIAL DYNAMICS

So far we have ignored the dynamic or time-varying aspects of actions — their growth, fluctuations, and change. The only exception to this is our discussion of action complexes in Chapter 3. There we defined a proceeding as a temporally ordered sequence of activities and stressed the role of organizations of Lindenmayer type in the generation and analysis or proceedings. However, such organizations do not by themselves suffice to account for the dynamic aspects of actions. Norms, which are the constituents of organizations, must be combined with other elements if they are to affect conduct in the way decided and prescribed. For example, a norm, as we know, attaches a task to a condition and it is evident that the norm subject must be informed that the condition obtains, if the norm is to be applied and action modified in accordance with the norm. In this chapter we shall study the factors whose combinations produce growth, fluctuation and change as components of feedback systems. Thus the central concept of cybernetics, namely that of an information-feedback control loop, will dominate our exposition in this chapter. The emphasis will be on the dynamic aspects of interactions and, hence, on the dynamic aspects of actions in the context of social systems; 'social dynamics' seems an appropriate indication of this form of interest.

41. INFORMATION-FEEDBACK CONTROL: AN EXAMPLE

It might be suggested that our language L is not suitable for an investigation into the time-varying aspects of action. There is some justification for this view. The modal operators which constitute the basic components of our conceptual framework have not been supplied with any temporal indices. And with the exception of the notion of a proceeding all of the concepts which have been defined in part or in full in terms of the basic concepts similarly lack temporal reference. For example, instead of saying that an agent brings it about at t that a state of affairs obtains at t' we have said, *tout court*, that he brings the state of affairs about. We have simplified matters in the same way by relying on 'a believes that p' rather than 'a believes at t that p at t''.

There are various ways of extending the syntax and semantics of L so as to make it suitable for the study of constructions with temporal reference.

(For some such extensions, see Kanger (1972), and Walton (1975).) We shall not now go on to select and elaborate on one such way, however. Motivated by a concern to keep the formal machinery relatively simple, we choose instead to use our constructions without temporal indices in contexts with a clearly understood, or clearly specified, temporal structure. We shall, as already indicated, describe these contexts in terms of information-feedback control loops. For this approach we are indebted to J. W. Forrester, who in seminal works (Forrester, 1961, 1968) has shown how it may be employed to yield adequate models of industrial and economic activity.

In his dynamic system models Forrester relies on three factors for the explanation of an industry's fluctuation and growth, *viz*. the structure of the system, amplification, and time delays. A typical example of his is that of a link in a multistage distribution system, say the link at retail level. The structure here is relatively simple: information about the retailer's inventory is conveyed to a manager, who converts the information into an order to a supplier to deliver a volume of goods into the inventory. Time delays may occur everywhere in this structure. That is to say, it may take some time to collect and transfer information about the inventory, some time for the manager to adjust the order to the supplier in the light of the information and the desired inventory, and some time for the supplier to deliver the goods into the inventory. Forrester's models adequately show how a system with such a structure may create amplifications of small retail sales changes because of the combined effects, within the system's structure, of time delays and managerial ordering policy. When placed in the more complex structure of cascaded inventories, these amplifications may lead to fluctuations in a factory production rate which are out of line with fluctuations in the actual consumer purchase rate. (For such an example, given in ample detail, see Forrester (1961, Chapter 2).)

Here we shall use an example drawn from another field, that of military battle. Let us imagine a mortar unit operating in wooded country. For the sake of simplicity we keep the unit small; it comprises, we assume, only three agents, a gunner, a signalman, and a leader or commander. Their task is to destroy a hostile machine-gun emplacement. The signalman is in a position to observe the bombs as they are dropped in the target area. He uses a field telephone to convey to the leader the points of impact of the projectiles and their distance from the target. On the basis of the information received from the signalman and, of course, the goal of having the machine-gun emplacement destroyed, the leader makes a decision, which he converts into an order to the gunner to aim and discharge the ordnance. This activity ceases if and when the target is hit, but may cease for other reasons.

This act situation has a structure which may quite easily be discerned from our description. The structure is that the leader converts an intention and a piece of information into an order to the gunner to aim and discharge the mortar; that the gunner executes the order, as a result of which a bomb is dropped in the target area; that the signalman compares the point of impact with the target point and indicates the interval between them to the leader; that the leader converts the new information into a new ordering decision, and so on. The structure may pretty plainly be thought of as a loop composed of a series of distinguished elements: actions done by the leader as decision-maker, by the gunner as executive or supplier, and by the signalman as collector and conveyor of information. If we generalize, we may say that the structure is the complex fact that a goal in union with some information results in an order, that the execution of the order results in a condition in the environment, that information about this condition is fed back to a decision-maker and influences his next ordering decision.

The loop structure has a well-defined temporal order. There is the interval of time during which the commander reaches a decision and converts it into an order to the gunner. This is followed by the interval during which the gunner executes the order. This is in turn followed by the time it takes for the bomb to reach the target area, which time, finally, as regards this particular cycle, is followed by the interval of time during which the signalman extracts information about the impact of the bomb and conveys the information collected to the commander.

Our example, obviously similar to examples of the kind favoured by Forrester, may readily be seen to be more complex than our description and provisional analysis of it suggest. We shall attend to the complexity later, but first we must emphasize a few points.

We have already said that information about the impact of a bomb, in relation to the target, is not instantaneously made available to the commander. It is equally important to note that the information need not be accurate or complete over the relevant range. In other words, information distortion is possible and we must therefore distinguish between the apparent and the actual condition of the environment — between the apparent and the actual level of the inventory. In some cases it is permissible to assume that the apparent and actual conditions are identical, or, which is the same, that the information contains no errors and that the collection and transfer of information are for all practical purposes instantaneous. But in general we must allow for the possibility that the information is distorted or, if not distorted, not available to reflect the present actual condition of the environment.

Secondly, the system described in our example is characterized by so-called negative feedback. That is to say, in making a decision the commander decides to counteract the deviation from a set target; for example, if in the immediately preceding cycle the gunner overshot the target, the commander does what he can to reduce the distance from the target, in that direction, in the next cycle. In other cases the system is not in this way deviation-counteracting but deviation-amplifying. The result of an action, which may be accidental and appear insignificant, is then increasingly amplified in such a way that deviation from an initial condition is increased with every cycle. Finally, some systems exhibit deviation-amplifying substructures and deviation-counteracting substructures, which together work to produce a complex overall pattern of dynamic behaviour.

42. ELEMENTARY INFORMATION-FEEDBACK CONTROL LOOPS

We have already indicated the main features of our model of dynamic behaviour: a goal in union with information about a condition of the environment is converted into an action, which changes the environment and thereby affects future decisions. In this and the following section we shall refine these features and attend to the complexity of the system described in our example.

An elementary information-feedback control loop comprises four stages: an inventory INV, an information system or inquiry stage IS, a goal formation stage GF, and a goal implementation stage GI. We think of each stage as an automaton. When an automaton cannot be fully specified or its complete specification is immaterial we use a well-known device of systems engineering and think of the automaton as a black box.

The four stages are connected in a cascade combination in the way shown by Figure 4.

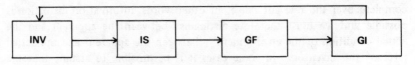

Fig. 4.   Elementary information-feedback control loop.

The cascade combination may be explained by applying it to the act situation of the commander in our example.

INV(a), the inventory available to a, is the information source of IS(a). The output of IS(a) is that a believes that the condition of INV(a) is as follows: the machine-gun emplacement was not destroyed by the previous bomb, the previous bomb fell short of the target by so many yards, and a is not at present issuing an order to the gunner. We let

(1) $B_a p$

represent this output. It constitutes an input to $GF(a)$. At this stage the transmission of wants and intentions takes place, involving the application of the principle of ideality and other principles of practical reasoning. Precisely what the components of $GF(a)$ are, and what practical reasoning occurs in $GF(a)$, are questions which we leave open. (Hence the black box. Its replacement by a white box, i.e. a system of known components in known relations to each other, is an important desideratum for the detailed explanation of a's action.) We assume only that the intention

(2) $B_a (p \supset \text{Shall } E_a q)$,

i.e. a's intention to issue an order to the gunner on the condition that p, is an element of $GF(a)$. Once (2) has been postulated,

(3) $B_a \text{ Shall } E_a q$,

which is a logical consequence of (1) and (2), may be thought of as an output of $GF(a)$. It forms in turn an input to $GI(a)$. As regards this stage, we postulate only the execution of intention (3), i.e. the action described by

(4) $E_a (B_a \text{ Shall } E_a q \supset E_a q)$.

We may now regard the action described by

(5) $E_a q$

as an output of $GI(a)$ and as an input to $INV(a)$. The new condition of $INV(a)$, which includes the circumstance that a has ordered the gunner to aim the mortar with the specified angle and direction of fire and to discharge it, constitutes an input to $IS(a)$. This means that a acquires information about what he is doing or has done, in which case not only (5) but also

(6) $B_a E_a q$

is true.

It may thus be seen that (1)–(6) can readily be fitted into the cascade combination of the four stages. In other words, a situation in which an agent intends to bring it about that q on the condition that p, believes that p is fulfilled, applies the unconditional intention to bring it about that q, and is convinced that he brings it about that q, may be articulated as an elementary information-feedback control loop. We shall here also accept the converse. That is to say, we shall always interpret an *elementary* information-feedback control loop in terms of a one-agent act situation of the kind described by (1)–(6).

It is of some interest to note that (6) follows logically from

(7) $B_a B_a$ Shall $E_a q$

and

(8) $B_a E_a (B_a$ Shall $E_a q \supset E_a q)$

according to the principles for B_a in our system L. (7) and (8) may, perhaps, be interpreted as saying that a is conscious of his intention and his execution of it — aware of the exercise of his will (cf. Section 15). If such consciousness is a universal feature of intentions and their execution, if, in other words,

(9) $(B_a$ Shall $E_a q \supset B_a B_a$ Shall $E_a q)$

and

(10) $(E_a (B_a$ Shall $E_a q \supset E_a q) \supset B_a E_a (B_a$ Shall $E_a q \supset E_a q))$

are true for any q and any a, then it may be said with full generality that the agent of an intentional action has the information that he performs the action (cf. Anscombe (1957), esp. Sections 5–7).

Can the claim that (9) and (10) are true for any q and any a be substantiated? One argument, possibly the strongest one, in support of the claim in respect of (9) is to the effect that every intention is formed in a decision, that every decision is made on the basis of deliberation, and that deliberation is a conscious mental activity or proceeding. An independent supporting argument is supplied by those who claim that

(11) $(B_a p \supset B_a B_a p)$

is logically true and hence also that (9) is logically true because it is an instance of (11). However, both arguments involve additional controversial considerations. In the absence of a comprehensive theory of mental action and consciousness all of these claims must, or so it seems to us, be rated as highly speculative. And the same, surely, must be said about the claim that (10) is true for any q and any a. Our account of the nature of an action is intended to be eminently general and, therefore, it is also intended to cover mental action, but in the absence of a reliable mark of the mental it cannot be used effectively in a discussion of, for example, the issues raised by (9) and (10).

43. A DYNAMIC SYSTEM MODEL

The cascade combination of four automata, which is represented in Figure 4 and which we used to describe the action of the commander in our example, may also be applied to the act situation of the gunner b and the signalman c. The action of the commander affects not only INV(a) but also INV(b). The latter is the information source of IS(b). An output of IS(b) is that b believes that a has ordered him to aim and discharge the mortar and that he is not at present carrying out the order; this is the counterpart of (1) in the commander's case. It forms an input to GF(b) which contains, as the counterpart of (2), b's intention to aim and discharge on the condition that he has been ordered to do so and is not at present doing so. An output of GF(b) is b's unconditional intention to aim and discharge — the counterpart of (3). It forms an input to GI(b), at which stage the intention is executed with the intended action as an output, giving the counterparts of (4) and (5), respectively. The output, finally, affects INV(b), thus completing an elementary loop in the case of b, and it affects INV(c), the information source of IS(c). The output of IS(c) is that c believes that the interval between the target point and the point of impact of the bomb dropped by b is such-and-such and that he is not now conveying that interval to a. This belief forms an input to GF(c), and so on.

The complexity of the dynamic action system described in our example now begins to emerge. It is made up of three interconnected elementary information-feedback control loops. The net, i.e. the elementary loops and their interconnections, is shown in Figure 5.

It might be argued that this figure though complex, still does not do justice to the complexity of the dynamic action under consideration. It might

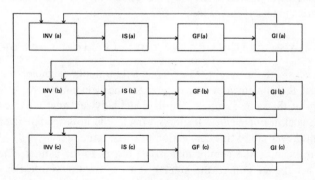

Fig. 5. Net of three elementary loops.

be argued, for example, that two elementary loops in adjunction are needed to bring out the structure of c's action. The first describes c's operation of an inquiring system, an act of seeking information, while the second loop describes the action by which c conveys the output of the inquiring system to the commander. There is no need now to make all such details explicit. Enough has been said to make the following description of our model of dynamic action intelligible.

We distinguish between nets and loops. A dynamic action is a net of one or more elementary information-feedback control loops. The loops are structurally identical and comprise four automata (an inventory, an information system, a goal formation stage, and a goal implementation stage) in cascade combination. Each elementary loop is closed in virtue of the fact that the output of goal implementation affects the inventory. The adjunction of loops in a net is always between the goal implementation of one loop and the inventory of another.

Structural features of nets may conveniently be studied with the aid of graph theory. This is so because we may think of a set of elementary loops as the vertex-set of a directed graph and of the set of connected loops as the arc-set of the graph, i.e. we may think of a net as a directed graph. Standard notions of graph theory, such as those of adjacent vertices, arc-sequences, paths, chains, circuits, etc., are therefore readily applicable. For example, a net is said to be connected if it is true, for any two loops f and g of the net, that there is a chain from f to g. Figure 5 represents a connected net. Given a connected net, we may define a non-elementary information-feedback control loop as a cascade combination of an inventory, an information system, a goal formation stage, and a goal implementation stage, not all of which are drawn from one and the same elementary loop. For example, the cascade combination of INV(a), GF(a), GI(b), and IS(c), in that order, constitutes a non-elementary loop.

44. APPLICATION OF THE MODEL TO N-AGENT ACTIONS

In the analysis of the system of dynamic action in our example we have said so far that the implementation of a goal in one elementary loop 'affects' the inventory of the same loop; and we have similarly said that the implementation of a goal in one elementary loop 'affects' the inventory of the adjacent loop. Can the nature of this connection be made more precise?

In our example the commander issues orders to the gunner. This means that he acts in relation to the gunner and delivers things into the gunner's inventory in the sense that he *brings about* states of affairs in that inventory.

This kind of connection is no doubt very common and, because $\models (E_a p \supset E_a E_a p)$, it is characteristic of the connection which closes an elementary loop, but we shall not insist on it as a general requirement. All that is required for a connection between two loops is that one agent act in consequence relation to another — that a condition of the inventory of one loop be a *consequence* of the implementation of a goal in another.

To illustrate this, consider a situation in which two agents have cooperated in relation to a third. Let us suppose that the cooperating agents have built a house for the third agent. It is not true of either agent that he alone built the house, nor is it true of either agent that the house would not have been delivered but for his action, for we may assume that the house might still have been delivered, as and when it was delivered, without the action of both. Assume it to be true of either agent, however, that but for his action the house might not have been delivered. In this situation the state of affairs that the third agent receives the house into his inventory is a consequence of things done by each of the cooperating agents. It would seem unduly restrictive to require that the connection between two loops always be an action in relation to an agent and thereby preclude the kind of case we have just considered from the field of n-agent dynamic actions. We shall therefore accept as a minimum requirement that the connection be an action in consequence relation to another agent. We thereby obtain what appears to be the weakest form of dependence in the adjunction between two loops that is definable in our general theory of action.

45. ELEMENTARY DYNAMICS

We shall now illustrate the proposed model of dynamic action in some detail. At the same time we refine the characterization of the model. We use examples which are simpler than the relatively complex example we used to introduce the model. To this end we first consider a system whose structure is that of one elementary loop. The *state* of the system at a given time is therefore specified in terms of four *state-variables*, namely the (state of the) inventory, information about the inventory, the formation of a goal or intention on the basis of the information and on the basis of factors which are not generated within the system, and, finally, implementation of the intention. The state of the system at a given time is specified by determining a value of each of these four variables.

The state of the inventory, we assume, is the distance between two objects X and Y. An agent regulates this distance by moving X along a line F. Thus

the inventory of the elementary loop may be represented as follows (cf.
MacKay (1968), p. 360):

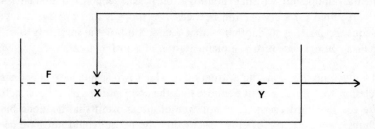

Fig. 6. State of the inventory of an elementary loop.

We assume that the agent's information about the state of the inventory,
the interval XY, is accurate, that collection of this information takes no
appreciable amount of time, and that collection is made every second. Also,
in the inquiring system of the loop the interval XY, the actual state of the
inventory, is compared with a fixed interval, called the *intended state* of the
inventory. More precisely, the inventory error or mismatch is the difference
between the intended and the actual state of the inventory. We assume that
the computation of the mismatch is accurate and takes no appreciable
amount of time, and we think of information about the mismatch as the
output of the inquiring system.

The intended distance of X from Y is, say, 100 units. That is to say, we
assume that the agent's intention is to keep X at a distance of 100 units from
Y. This intention is present in the goal-formation system of the loop as one of
its constant features. We also assume, as regards goal-formation, that there is
a regularity in the agent's intentions to correct the inventory error. In fact,
each time the agent intends to correct the error he intends to do so at the rate
of one 10th of the mismatch per second, 10 being, by assumption, the adjust-
ment time in seconds, i.e. the time it would take to correct the inventory
error if the current rate of correction was implemented (cf. Forrester (1968),
Section 2.2). This means that we assume, as another constant feature of the
goal-formation system, that the agent has a *policy* for the correction of the
mismatch, a policy which determines the correction rate he should use at any
given moment.

We think of the policy as a generalized intention. The agent has the policy
if and only if he believes that if the mismatch is n units large, then it shall be
the case that he moves X $n/10$ units along line F in the direction toward or

away from Y depending on whether X is too far away from or too close to Y. This belief may be expressed by a sentence of the form

(12) $B_a \forall x (p(x) \supset \text{Shall } E_a q(x))$.

That the policy determines the rate of correction at any one time means that the agent has a particular intention of type (2) because he has the generalized intention just described. In other words, it means that a particular intention exists as a result of transmission of intention.

We assume, finally, that the execution of the intention which is the output of the goal-formation stage takes place every second and has, for all practical purposes, an instantaneous effect on the interval XY. If the state of the system at a given moment is known, the next state of the system can be determined, and given that this state has been determined, its immediate successor can be determined, and so on. To illustrate, we let the state of the system at time 0 be: the interval XY is 0 units, the agent is informed that the mismatch is 100 units, he intends to correct the discrepancy at the rate of 10 units per second, and he executes this intention. The state of the system at time 1 will then be: the interval XY is 10 units, the agent is informed that the mismatch is 90 units, he intends to correct the discrepancy at the rate of 9 units per second, and he executes this intention. And at time 2 the system will be in the following state: the interval XY is 19 units, the agent is informed that the mismatch is 81 units, he intends to correct the mismatch at the rate of 8.1 units per second, and he executes this intention. Each state-description is to the effect that the agent intentionally corrects a known inventory error at the rate of one 10th of the error. A sequence of state-descriptions specifies how the system changes during an interval of time – it describes a complex action as a time-varying process.

46. Two-agent dynamic action

The abstract structure just considered is very simple. We next make it fractionally more complex by adding a second agent, a supplier b who receives orders from an agent a to move X in relation to Y along line F. This means that the structure of the system now to be considered is that of two linked elementary loops, one for each agent. And this in turn means that the state of the system at a given time is specified in terms of two sets of four state-variables, the four that are characteristic of each loop.

As regards the loop that characterizes a's action, we make the following assumptions: a's information about the state of the inventory is accurate, collecting it is for all practical purposes instantaneous, and collection is made, say, every third second; a intends to have the distance between X and Y kept at 100 units, and his policy is to supply b with orders for correction of the mismatch at the rate of one 10th of the mismatch per second, i.e. a's policy is to create units on order at the rate of 10 units per second.

We make the corresponding information assumptions about the loop that characterizes b's action. We assume in addition that b's policy is that of filling a's orders, at the rate of, say, one 10th of the units on order per second. Given an initial state description, we may now compute the description of every subsequent state of the system. Let the state of the system at time 0 be: the interval XY is 0 units, a is informed that the mismatch is 100 units, a intends to order and orders 10 units per second; b has an order stock of 100 units, is informed that the mismatch is 100 units, and intends to deliver and delivers 10 units per second. The state of the system at time 3 will then be: the interval XY is 30 units, a is informed that the mismatch is 70 units, and a intentionally orders 7 units per second; b has an order stock of 100 units, is informed that the mismatch is 100 units, and intentionally delivers 10 units per second. And at time 12 the state of the system will be in round figures: the interval XY is 110 units, a is informed that X is 10 units too far away from Y, and he intentionally orders a reduction of 1 unit per second; b has an order stock of 57 units and he fills the orders at the rate of 6 units per second. (A similar but more elaborate example together with a graphic representation of the computed details may be found in Forrester (1968, Section 2.3).)

Our example has been constructed in such a way that there soon develops, as the dynamic action progresses, a difference between a's ordering rate and b's delivery rate, which is equal to a's receiving rate. Because of this difference b's correction of the error in a's inventory will not smoothly secure the intended inventory, as is the case in the example presented in the previous section, but will overshoot and oscillate around the intended state of a's inventory. Thus a sequence of state-descriptions specifies how the system changes and fluctuates.

The case of social dynamics just considered is of course a very simple one, involving, as it does, only two agents. But generalization on the basis of what was said in Sections 43 and 44 to systems of more than two agents is obvious and immediate, and, also, the importance of the two-agent case should not be underrated, if what we said in Section 39 about the relevance of two-agent interaction for the understanding of social groups, social systems, and social orders is correct.

In the sample system of social dynamics which we used to introduce our dynamic system model, cooperation between the three agents — the commander, the gunner, and the signalman – may be assumed to be to the advantage of each of them. In this case we may also assume that cooperation is most likely to occur because the advantage to be had from cooperation is likely to rank so high for each agent as to make deviation a very unattractive action alternative. In other words, the sample system has to a large extent the character of a pure coordination game and it may be said, in the language of game theory, that the organization concerned is made up of cooperative equilibrium policies. In cases at the other extreme, cases of strict opposition, the interests of the parties involved deviate so radically that no gain may be obtained from cooperation; here cooperation is not only unlikely to occur because of the radically opposed interests of the parties – it can hardly be given a well-defined or coherent meaning.

In the sequel we shall consider the dynamic system model in the context of dynamic social action which is neither of the type pure coordination nor of the type strict opposition, but of type Prisoner's Dilemma. In act situations of this kind cooperation between two parties is potentially very beneficial to both, but it is unlikely to occur, at least initially, because of the opposition of the interests of the parties. The study of organizations made up of equilibrium policies for such situations is important in view of their prevalence in social life. The analytical tools for this study are supplied by the theory of games or interdependent decision, which has a most natural application in social dynamics.

47. INTERDEPENDENT DECISION

We consider a structure described in game-theoretic terms. The basic structure is a temporally ordered sequence of choice situations of the Prisoner's Dilemma type. In each choice situation two parties compete for certain benefits or pay-offs by selecting one of two alternatives, C (cooperation) and D (deviation). If both choose alternative C, each gains a benefit of 1 unit; if both choose D, they lose 1 unit each; and if they choose incongruously, the D strategist receives 4 units at the expense of the C strategist who has to take a loss of 3 units in this case. We may summarize this in customary matrix form:

TABLE V

A Prisoner's Dilemma

		Player b		
		C	D	Row minima
Player a	C	1,1	−3,4	−3
	D	4,−3	−1,−1	−1
Column minima		−3	−1	

This matrix shows in detail how *a* and *b* are interdependent. The nature of their interdependence may be further emphasized by means of the net represented in Figure 7.

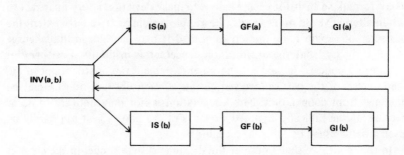

Fig. 7.   Prisoner's Dilemma as two connected loops.

The two players have a joint inventory. Neither player is able on his own to determine his share of the goods in the inventory. This means of course also that a player is unable to make the other player choose a certain alternative. Their interdependence is genuine: actions by both determine the volume of goods in the inventory and the share of them that accrues to a player at any one time.

The players possess the information encoded in Table V and Figure 7, but a player does not know which alternative his opponent is going to select on any occasion of choice. We may therefore assume that the players make their selections simultaneously. However, information about choices already made is conveyed to both players in, we assume, the form of knowledge of the pay-offs gained as a result of these choices.

The players are maximizers. More precisely, the goal of each player is to accumulate for himself as many units of benefit as possible. The application of the axiom of rationality (see Section 40) is therefore simple and immediate; a player acts rationally on a given choice occasion if he selects the alternative which yields the greater benefit (smaller loss). So what does a player do if he acts rationally? He chooses D. For if his competitor chooses C, he is better off with D, and if his competitor chooses D, alternative D is again more attractive. So D is better regardless of the choice made by the competitor, i.e. rationality dictates the choice of D. It is not surprising, then, that (D, D) is an equilibrium pair, the only such pair, in fact, of the game. That is to say, *a* prefers the outcome of (D, D) to that of (C, D) and, conversely, *b* prefers the outcome of (D, D) to that of (D, C). Accordingly, a player cannot possibly improve his position by abandoning his equilibrium strategy if his opponent does not abandon his equilibrium strategy. The choice of the equilibrium strategy by both players — joint rationality — results in a loss of one unit for each in each round, a loss which should be compared with the gain of one unit each under joint irrationality.

The game has a risk, a temptation, and a gain aspect, in terms of which its character as a dilemma may be further elucidated. The game represented in Table V is an instance of the structure shown in Table VI, where the pay-offs are subject to the constraints that $\delta < \beta < \alpha < \gamma$ and the constraint that $\gamma + \delta < 2\alpha$:

TABLE VI

General structure of the Prisoner's Dilemma

		Player b	
		C	D
Player a	C	α, α	δ, γ
	D	γ, δ	β, β

By playing noncooperatively each player can guarantee himself at least β. If a player chooses the cooperative strategy and trusts his opponent to do the same, he may get δ, the worst outcome. Thus, the risk he runs by trusting his opponent is the difference β-δ. The gain, or reward for cooperation, is the difference α-β. The difference γ-α, finally, is the temptation to choose the noncooperative strategy hoping that the opponent will choose to cooperate. In the game shown in Table V the risk, the gain, and the temptation are 2, 2, and 3 units, respectively.

In experimental work with the Prisoner's Dilemma it has been shown that, in the absence of communication between the players, cooperation tends to decrease as the risk and the temptation increase and increase as the gain increases. This is not surprising when one considers that increasing the risk and the temptation of the game makes it resemble one of strict opposition, whereas increasing the gain makes it resemble more and more a game of pure coordination. However, when the game lies between these two extremes its character of a dilemma is the fact that, as we have already said, following Bonacich (1970) and Nurmi (1975), that cooperation between the parties is beneficial for each of them but is unlikely to occur, at least initially, because of the opposition of their interests.

All of this is well-known and requires no comments. We next extend the basic game in order to make it more relevant for the study of social dynamics.

48. INTERDEPENDENT DECISION: METAGAMES

Having thus seen that it does not always pay to be rational the players of the Prisoner's Dilemma game are forced to ask themselves whether they should be rational. Howard (1966a) has shown that if the players are given leave to ask this question, the basic game is pregnant with interesting possibilities. In the *theory* of rational choice the leave is given in the form of the axiom of free will (see Section 40). Without this axiom the theory of rational choice is exhausted by the axiom of rationality. The application of the theory of the Prisoner's Dilemma then yields, as is shown in the standard analysis of the game which we reviewed in the previous section, the result that there is just one rational strategy in the game, namely that of always choosing D. However, with the introduction of the axiom of free will the situation changes, for a player is then free to act or not to act in accordance with the axiom of rationality. This freedom must be taken into account in the specification of the strategies available to the players. In the basic game there are two strategies open to each player; this is a brute fact which remains unaltered. But once the axiom of free will has been introduced, new games may be defined given the basic game as a point of departure. The new games are called metagames and they have a very natural interpretation. The application of the axiom of rationality to the metagames need not and, in fact, does not give the same result as its application to the basic game.

The first metagame for player b, the b-metagame, is defined by the matrix as shown in Table VII.

TABLE VII

b-metagame in the Prisoner's Dilemma

		Player b				
		C/C	C/D	D/C	D/D	Row minima
Player a	C	1,1	1,1	−3,4	−3,4	−3
	D	4,−3	−1,−1	4,−3	−1,−1	−1
	Column minima	−3	−1	−3	−1	

Here X/Y is b's metastrategy of choosing X if a chooses C and Y if a chooses D. For example, C/C is b's metastrategy of choosing C regardless of a's choice. The pair (C, C/C) will clearly give the pay-off of the pair (C, C) in the basic game.

The strategies in the b-metagame may naturally be interpreted as *policies*, i.e. as rules or norms for making choices in the basic game. As all norms, the policies are conditional in character; they make b's task of choosing C or D conditional on a's choice of C or D. The four possible policies are not all equally acceptable. Player *b* answers the question of which policy to choose on the basis of the axiom of rationality, and, of course, player *a* answers the question of whether to choose C or D on the same basis. Inspection of Table VII reveals that (D, D/D) is the unique equilibrium pair of the *b*-metagame. Because of the perfect symmetries of the basic game the *a*-metagame is entirely parallel, definable by means of a 4 × 2 matrix and having (D/D, D) as its unique equilibrium pair. Now (D, D/D) = (D/D, D) = (D, D), so at the first metalevel joint rationality is still less rewarding than joint irrationality. It makes no difference, in terms of pay-offs, whether or not they play games at the first metalevel in addition to the basic game. However, this does not mean that no progress has been made. For once the games at the first metalevel have been defined, games at the next level are definable in virtue of the axiom of free will. In the *a-b*-metagame *a* has to choose between policies which make *a*'s choice of C or D conditional on *b*'s choice of policy. We may represent the *a-b*-metagame in the way as shown in Table VIII.

TABLE VIII

a-b-metagame in the Prisoner's Dilemma

	C/C	C/D	D/C	D/D	Row minima
C/C/C/C	1,1	1,1	-3,4	-3,4	-3
C/C/C/D	1,1	1,1	-3,4	-1,-1	-3
C/C/D/C	1,1	1,1	4,-3	-3,4	-3
C/C/D/D	1,1	*1,1*	4,-3	-1,-1	*-1*
C/D/C/C	1,1	-1,-1	-3,4	-3,4	-3
C/D/C/D	1,1	-1,-1	-3,4	-1,-1	-3
C/D/D/C	1,1	-1,-1	4,-3	-3,4	-3
C/D/D/D	1,1	-1,-1	4,-3	-1,-1	*-1*
D/C/C/C	4,-3	1,1	-3,4	-3,4	-3
D/C/C/D	4,-3	1,1	-3,4	-1,-1	-3
D/C/D/C	4,-3	1,1	4,-3	-3,4	-3
D/C/D/D	4,-3	*1,1*	4,-3	-1,-1	*-1*
D/D/C/C	4,-3	-1,-1	-3,4	-3,4	-3
D/D/C/D	4,-3	-1,-1	-3,4	-1,-1	-3
D/D/D/C	4,-3	-1,-1	4,-3	-3,4	-3
D/D/D/D	4,-3	-1,-1	4,-3	*-1,-1*	*-1*
Column minima	-3	*-1*	-3	*-1*	

In Table VIII X/Y/Z/W stands for the following policy: choose X if *b* chooses C/C, Y if he chooses C/D, Z if he chooses D/C, and W if he chooses D/D. To illustrate the computation of the pay-offs consider the policy pair (C/D/C/C, D/C). *a*'s choice determines the selection of C when *b* chooses D/C. But if *a* chooses C, *b*'s policy dictates the choice of D. So the policy pair in question has the pay-off of the pair (C, D) in the basic game.

The a-b-metagame has three equilibria, namely (i) (D/D/D/D, D/D), (ii) (D/C/D/D, C/D), and (iii) (C/C/D/D, C/D). Pair (i) may be termed a non-cooperative equilibrium because the application of its two policies results in the non-cooperative strategy pair (D, D) in the basic game. Pairs (ii) and (iii), by contrast, are cooperative equilibria; both lead to (C, C) in the basic game. Pair (i) does not compare favourably with (ii) or (iii). Player a cannot possibly lose by abandoning his non-cooperative policy D/D/D/D in favour of D/C/D/D, or C/C/D/D, but he may gain. So rationality dictates the selection of one of these policies. If b now responds rationally, (ii) or (iii) will ensue. Thus the a-b-metagame yields a larger set of basic equilibria than the basic game or the first-level metagames. For reason of symmetry the b-a-metagame may be seen to yield the same set of basic equilibria, but in other cases the sets of basic equilibria that result from equilibria of metagames need not intersect. In Howard (1966b) it is shown that the set of basic equilibria in a two-person game does not grow after the second metalevel.

In the a-b-metagame b has just one cooperative equilibrium strategy, namely C/D or tit-for-tat: to cooperate exactly when a cooperates. In the same game a has two cooperative equilibrium strategies. These differ with respect to the strategy C/C of simple-minded cooperativeness. Under C/C/D/D it is immaterial for the opponent whether he follows C/D or C/C. In other words, simple-minded cooperativeness is allowed in this case, whereas under D/C/D/D it will incur a heavy penalty. A switch by a from C/C/D/D to D/C/D/D may therefore be thought of as a punishment for simple-minded cooperativeness (cf. Nurmi (1975), pp. 13–14).

The above analysis of the Prisoner's Dilemma in the theory of metagames shows clearly how this theory may be used to study the policy components of dynamic systems involving two (or more) agents. The theory may be applied to find equilibrium organizations, i.e. organizations comprising policies which the players have no reason to abandon as long as their opponents do not abandon them. When used in this way the theory is a powerful tool in the study of properties of systems of social dynamics.

49. METAGAMES AND INCOMPLETE INFORMATION

The fact that there is a cooperative solution to the Prisoner's Dilemma does not mean that the solution will be reached in practice as a matter of course. Whether the solution is reached or not depends on contingencies involving threat, trust, the extent of information, reliable communication and other factors.

Metagames often have the character of games with incomplete information.

This is due to the fact that information about a basic game and the state of play in such a game at a given time is frequently compatible with the supposition of the pursuit of any of a number of different policies. Observing a choice in a basic game need give no firm evidence about choice at some metalevel. This circumstance, which obviously has dynamic consequences, may easily be illustrated.

Assume that the Prisoner's Dilemma game described in Table V is played repeatedly. On each occasion of choice both players make their selections and before the next choice they learn of the pay-offs they secured in the previous choice. We may assume that they are in a position to 'metacommunicate', i.e. to comment on the game as it progresses, to proclaim that a policy is being implemented, to propose that a policy be pursued, and so on. These comments, however, are words, but in a battle the parties involved may be wary of taking words at their face value. The only firm information available concerns the pay-offs in past choices. This, as far as it goes, and the words, as far as they go, constitute the only evidence the players have concerning the policy of the opponent.

Let it be that both players play non-cooperatively in an opening series of choices. They lose one unit each and conclude that they are indeed playing non-cooperatively. Player a, in particular, concludes that (D/D/D/D, D/D) in the a-b-metagame is being implemented. He ascertains and proclaims that he has nothing to lose by switching to D/C/D/D. The opponent, likewise, realizes that he has nothing to lose by switching to C/D. He effects the change and the mutually favourable outcome $(1, 1)$ is obtained. The players now make words in praise of cooperation and its value: 'in a difficult situation of this sort it always pays to cooperate'. Player b, keen as always to maximize his gain, imposes an optimistic interpretation on all of this. He takes the favourable outcome and the encouraging words as an indication that a is playing C/C/C/C. That is to say, he attributes C/C/C/C to a, and this attribution is certainly compatible with the outcome $(1, 1)$ that is currently being recorded. He therefore switches to D/D in an attempt to profit from a's willingness to cooperate unconditionally, only to discover that his attribution of policy to a was mistaken. a concludes that trusting b makes him vulnerable and that b is therefore not to be trusted, tells b that if 'this is the way you are going to treat me, don't expect any cooperation', and switches back to D/D/D/D. b is now apologetic, saying that he misunderstood a's talk about the value of cooperation and implements a proclaimed return to C/D. a is insulted to think that b took him to be simple-minded enough to play C/C/C/C. So he continues to play D/D/D/D and the outcome, $(-1, -1)$, stays the same. It is therefore true, for all that *a* knows, that *b* is still playing non-cooperatively; in fact, every affirmation by *b* that he is playing tit-for-tat tends to confirm *a*'s attribution of the policy of non-cooperation to *b* — 'it's exactly as I thought, he can't be trusted'. However, after a cooling-off period *a* realizes, as before, that D/C/D/D is his best policy and switches to this. But, disenchanted with the idea of cooperating without any increase in pay-off, *b* has meanwhile returned to D/D. There is now but one conclusion for *a* to draw: '*b* is not cooperating, I was right all the time'. This, clearly, is the stuff of which gruesome twosomes, double-binds and split personalities can be made.

50. TELEOLOGICAL SYSTEMS

According to the view expressed in Section 42 an elementary information-feedback control loop exists if and only if an agent intends to bring it about that *q* on the condition that *p*, believes that *p* is fulfilled, applies the unconditional intention to bring it about that *q*, and is convinced that that is what he does. We have suggested that a complex fact of this kind be structured as a cascade combination of four automata, an inventory or environment, an inquiring system, a goal-formation unit, and a goal-implementation unit. It may be said, more generally, that systems of the kind we have studied in this chapter exist if and when one or more goals or intentions are implemented in the light of information about an environment, which is in part determined by the fact that those goals are implemented. Such systems may be termed *teleological* for obvious reasons. All teleological systems are systems of mutual causal processes and systems with feedback and as such they are cybernetic systems. We shall not argue the convernse, namely that all cybernetic systems are also teleological.

We consider a cybernetic system of a well-known kind, a thermostat arrangement for regulating the temperature in a room. Changes in temperature cause a curved rod to curl or uncurl slightly. These movements cause an attached straight rod which is pivoted at one end to move at the other end and as the rod moves it opens or closes an electric circuit. Closing the circuit starts a heater, which affects the temperature in the room, whereas opening the circuit stops the heater.

It would be entirely in accord with common practice in cybernetics and control engineering to describe the thermostat arrangement in the following way. The relevant state of the inventory is the temperature in the room. The curved rod is a thermometer and as such an inquiring system which collects information about the inventory and computes the difference between the actual room temperature and a standard or preferred or intended temperature. The straight rod receives this information and converts it into an order to the heater to start or stop heating the room. Or, to take another well-known illustration, we might use the language of our example in Section 45 to describe the way a toilet water tank works thus: the interval XY is the level or volume of water in the tank, a float collects information about the interval XY and computes the difference between this interval and a preferred interval – the water level of a full tank. A shaft connecting the float with a valve orders the valve to correct the mismatch at the rate of one-tenth of the mismatch per second. And, finally, the valve executes this order.

To describe the thermostat or the water tank in this way in the idioms of information-feedback control loops, as understood here, may be innocuous and useful as a *façon de parler*. But should it be regarded as anything more than that? Does the thermostat really have beliefs about the temperature in the room? Does it really intend to keep the temperature within certain limits? Does it really order the heater to start or stop heating the room? Do the thermostat and the water tank exhibit goal-directed or purposive activities?

It cannot be denied that there is an important similarity between servo-mechanisms, such as the thermostat or the water tank, and teleological systems, i.e. agents who form intentions and knowingly execute these in the light of their beliefs about the environment in which they act and about the effect of their actions on the environment. We have in fact relied on a similarity when we have borrowed ideas from cybernetics for use in the analysis of human action. However, in doing so we have tacitly assumed that the similarity in question is best captured by the statement that servo-mechanisms and teleological systems are all cybernetic systems, systems with causal feedback loops. We also think that the cascade combination of four automata captures the similarity at a fairly fundamental level. Thus, the similarity consists in the fact that the systems are causal structures of one and the same kind and not in the circumstance that the elements of this structure are elements of the same kind. So understood the similarity can be affirmed without commitment to any views which entail that human beings are essentially like extremely complex toilet water tanks or that toilet water tanks are essentially like exceedingly simple human beings.

We have borrowed ideas from cybernetics because we think that this is a science which makes substantial contributions to the understanding of complex causal structures and which can therefore be expected to contribute to the understanding of human action, especially in its dynamic aspect. There is no need, however, to repay this loan by accepting, for example, the conception that servomechanisms are intrinsically purposeful. (For such conceptions and criticisms of them, see the papers collected in Buckley (1968, Part V, Section A). See also Sommerhoff (1969).)

We have given intentional action a central place in our account of dynamic action. In answer to the question of how much of our conduct is intentional, a number of philosophers have claimed that all human action is intentional. If this is understood to mean that all act relations are relations of acting intentionally, the claim is clearly mistaken for, as for example Goldman (1970, p. 17) has pointed out, there are actions, such as miscalculating, which preclude the corresponding intentions. Because of the existence of such act relations not every act instance can be intentional either. But the claim can be understood differently; it can be understood to mean that whenever an agent acts in relation to an individual then he acts intentionally in relation to some individual or other. Suppose, for example, that a boy unintentionally moves some gravel on a garden path. If the claim is correct, the boy at the time also acts intentionally in relation to some individual – he is intentionally chasing a dog along the garden path, or he intentionally walks to his favourite spot in the garden, or he intentionally takes a short cut to the neighbour's house, etc. In this way one can speak of the omnipresence of intentions in acting without commitment to the view that every act instance is intentional.

The 'thesis of intentionality', understood in the second way, is probably mistaken. For assume that the boy moves some gravel on the garden path while walking in his sleep. In this case it is highly unlikely that the boy would be acting intentionally in relation to some individual or other. And yet he moves the gravel.

CHAPTER 6

ACTION-EXPLANATIONS

A central aim of scientific activity is to explain phenomena. In the case of
social science the explanation of human action must be a central concern
because of the nature of social reality. In this chapter, which concludes our
work, we explore some patterns of action-explanations. We first attend to a
distinction between understanding and knowledge of facts. This constitutes
the *fundamentum divisionis* of the classification of explanations as essential
and connective explanations. The latter include causal explanations as an
important subcategory. The interrelations of these categories and their
application to action is discussed in some detail. No attempt is made to
explore all aspects of action-explanations. For example, we ignore problems
concerning the testing of hypotheses.

51. UNDERSTANDING AND KNOWLEDGE OF FACTS

An important organizing principle in this chapter is the distinction between
understanding and knowledge of facts. To introduce it we consider a few
examples of competence, i.e. the possession of abilities by individuals.
Consider first a child who can sort objects into two classes: those that are red
and those that are not red. A red object may be said to satisfy or be a positive
instance of the colour property red and, similarly, an object that is not red
may be said to fail to satisfy or be a negative instance of the colour. In this
terminology we may describe the child's ability by saying that he can classify
objects correctly as positive or negative instances of the property red. He
occasionally makes a mistake, for example when the conditions under which
he is observing the objects are abnormal. But his competence is clearly
compatible with a defective performance which is due in this way to limitations and constraints imposed by contingent circumstances.

We consider, secondly, a child who has learnt to order objects that are not
too heavy for him to lift in respect of weight. When presented with two such
objects the child places them in the opposite pans of a balance; if the balance
remains in equilibrium the child takes the objects to be of equal weight, and
in all other cases he takes the object in the pan which sinks to be heavier than
the object in the pan which rises. We may describe the child's competence
thus: he can correctly classify pairs of objects in a certain class as positive or

negative instances of the relations of having the same weight and of being heavier than.

We consider next a pupil who can compute the sum of two integers with different signs. When asked to find the sum of two such integers he first finds the difference of their absolute values and then prefixes this number with the sign of the integer having the greatest absolute value. In this case we describe the pupil's ability by saying that he can correctly classify triples of integers as positive or negative instances of the relation of being the sum of two integers with different signs.

We consider, finally, the following case. The son of a home engineer has often observed his father at work and thereby learnt to recognize certain complex arrangements of pipes, boilers, tanks, cylinders, valves, pumps, thermostats, etc. as hot water heating systems. Confronted with various arrangements of the relevant kind he quickly discovers what sort of instance each one of them is: 'here we have a gravity feed because it lacks a circulation pump', 'this can't be a gravity feed because of the small tubing', 'this is a pumped system with an injector tee', and so on. In short, the son correctly classifies complex arrangements of a certain kind as positive or negative instances of certain types of system.

In each of these examples an individual may be said to *know how* to classify more or less complex elements as positive or negative instances of certain relations. (As before we count properties as one-place relations.) The force of this description is exactly the same as the force of the description already used. We shall say more briefly, in each example, that an individual knows the nature (type, kind, class, etc.) of certain elements or, still more briefly, that he *understands* certain relations. In our first example, a child understands the colour red; in our second example, a child understands the relation that an object bears to another just in case it has the same weight as or is heavier than the second; in our third example, a pupil understands (the relation of being) the sum of two integers with different signs; and in our fourth example, the son of a home engineer understands the gravity feed.

Knowing how to classify elements should be distinguished from knowing that something is the case. Knowledge of fact cannot, as every student of philosophy knows, be identified with true opinion. If true opinion is to count as knowledge it must have been arrived at by means of a reliable method, i.e. acquired as the result of applying a procedure which gives, at least, greater than random success. For example, if a true opinion is formed on the basis of conclusive evidence, it certainly counts as knowledge. But a true opinion formed on the basis of non-conclusive evidence may still count as knowledge; whether it counts as knowledge or not depends on the reliability of the inquiring system used to collect the evidence. Greater than random success seems to be a minimum requirement of reliability.

Thus, knowledge that something is the case is a true opinion which is salient in some way. It is not certain that salience here can be characterized once and for all in terms of a specific procedure or type of inquiring system. If this is correct, all we can say in general is that the salience of a true opinion which constitutes knowledge that something is the case consists in the fact that it realizes an ideal, that the true opinion is justified, as many writers on the theory of knowledge have stressed, that it is based on acceptable evidence, or that its bearer has a right to hold it. For example, there can be no doubt that an ideal is realized by a's believing that p on the basis of conclusive evidence, i.e. evidence which is such that no increase of a's body of evidence will force a to abandon his opinion that p. But on the other hand it is plain, as we have already indicated, that not all epistemic ideals are grounded on considerations pertaining to conclusive evidence. That the fact that a believes that p realizes an ideal may be expressed in our language L by means of sentences of the form $(B_a p \ \& \ \text{Ought} \ B_a p)$. If we now add the requirement that a's belief be true, we have in fact a characterization of a's knowledge that p which we may state in the form of the following definition:

(Df22) $K_a p = (p \ \& \ B_a p \ \& \ \text{Ought} \ B_a p)$

(The idea formulated in (Df22) is not new. See, for example, Chisholm (1955–56).) Although the elaboration of this conception of knowledge may not be altogether unproblematic, there can hardly be any doubt as to its viability. Nor do we think that there can be any doubt as to the viability of the distinction between understanding of relations and knowledge of facts.

That we wish to distinguish between understanding thought of as a skill and knowledge of a fact thought of as an ideal true belief, should not be construed as the suggestion that the two can be separated in practice. This is not something we wish to suggest. It is probably true that every exercise of practical understanding requires knowledge of some fact or facts and, conversely, that practical understanding is necessary for the acquisition of knowledge of a fact. For example, in order to show by means of a calculation that $-10 + 8 = -2$ and thus acquire knowledge of this fact, is it not necessary that one should understand the sum of two integers with different signs? And, similarly, since understanding the sum of two such integers is the ability to make certain calculations, is it not necessary for the exercise of this ability that one should know some facts, e.g. that $|-10| = 10$, i.e. that the absolute value $|-10|$ of -10 is 10? However, that understanding and knowledge of facts are, or may be, mutually dependent or complementary in this way does of course not mean that they can be conceptually identified. Knowledge of facts, as the expression we use to refer to this kind of knowledge makes clear, pertains to facts, whereas understanding is knowledge of the nature of things and as such pertains to the relational elements of facts.

52. UNDERSTANDING AND KNOWLEDGE OF INTENTIONS AND ACTIONS

Everything we said in the previous section is applicable to actions and agents. We understand the dyadic relation of kicking if and only if we know how to classify pairs of individuals as positive or negative instances of kicking. When we understand the relation we classify as negative instances, for example, pairs (x, y) of individuals such that x strikes y with his hand. Similarly, we understand the intention to kick if and only if we know how to classify agents as positive or negative instances of the property anyone has just in case he intends to kick somebody. And again, we understand the relation of kicking somebody intentionally if and only if we know how to classify as positive or negative instances pairs (x, y) of individuals such that x kicks y intentionally, i.e. makes his action in relation to y conform to his intention to kick y. And so on.

Thus, from the logical point of view, understanding an act relation or an agent as the carrier of an intention is not in principle different from understanding a relation of some other type or from understanding the nature of an individual of some other kind. The same may be said about knowledge of actions and intentions. There are important differences in practice, however. These are entirely due to the fact that intentions cannot be defined in terms of observable overt behavior alone. This has been argued convincingly by Taylor (1950) on the ground that one and the same behaviour pattern can be consistent with the supposition of any of a variety of *completely different* intentions. To take an example not used by Taylor, there is no end to the number of intentions to indicate that something is the case with which the act of raising one's arm, say, can be done. In other cases the variability is more restricted, but this in no way undermines the soundness of the argument that, though observable behaviour gives evidence of intentions, these cannot be defined in terms of such behaviour alone.

It is true, conversely, that most intentions have no unique manifestations in overt, external behaviour, if, indeed, they have any such manifestations at all. There is in principle no limit to the actions by means of which one might manifest the intention to indicate that some one state of affairs obtains. There are, again, cases where this variability is more restricted; the carnal connection of a singing master with a junior pupil can hardly be taken to manifest the intention to train the pupil's voice (cf. R. v. Williams [1923] 1 Q.B. 340), but, whatever the variability, the main point stands, *viz*. that intentions are internal properties of agents which have in general no tight connections with directly observable behaviour. This creates difficulties for the exercise of our understanding of and for the acquisition of knowledge of intentions and, *a fortiori*, actions. This last point, which concerns the relevance for understanding and knowledge of actions, of the way intentions enter into actions, is worth some elaboration.

Consider the relation that x bears to y just in case x sets himself to kick y. This relation is distinct from the relation of kicking, and understanding the former is one thing and understanding the latter another thing. Understanding the relation of kicking intentionally is different again; it obviously requires understanding of agents who intend to kick for the relation concerned is in fact the restriction of the relation of setting oneself to kick to that class of agents. The further restriction of this (restricted) relation to the class of agents who intend to kick because they intend to defend themselves is the relation of kicking in self-defence. We may speak of understanding it in terms of understanding kicking as a necessary and/or sufficient means to self-defence as an end and what we have knowledge of here is of intending agents of yet another type. Restricting the relation of kicking intentionally to the class of agents who intend to kick because they intend to defend a friend against assault yields a different relation. Understanding it is a matter of understanding kicking as a means to the end of defending a friend against assault.

In short, the means-end bifurcation of act relations makes evident, with all desirable force, the way intentions enter into the constitution of some act relations. The exercise of our understanding of and the acquisition of knowledge of some act relations are therefore beset by the same difficulties as those we referred to above in connection with understanding and knowledge of intention.

53. MEANING AND UNDERSTANDING

Understanding is often thought of as linked to meaning; understanding, it might be said, is knowledge of meaning, and not, as we have suggested in the two previous sections, a matter of knowing how to classify elements. In view of this we must say something about meaning, if only to further clarify our notion of understanding.

The question 'What do you mean to do?' has exactly the same force as

'What do you intend to do?'. A meaning, in this sense of the word, is something intended, the 'object' of some intention. 'I mean to make hay tomorrow if there is sunshine' might answer the question by making clear that making hay when there is sunshine is what a person intends to do. We shall not use the words 'mean' and 'meaning' in this very general sense, for 'intend' and its derivatives serve perfectly well here. We shall reserve 'meaning' for the objects of intentions of a select kind, namely *intentions to indicate* (to somebody) that something is the case (cf. Section 36). With 'When I spoke, this way my meaning' the speaker clarifies what he intended to indicate in an earlier speech act. The nature of intentions to indicate can be further elucidated by means of the notion of reference. If a indicates to b that he is on speed trials, one of the things he does is that he refers to himself and another thing he does is that he refers to the property of being on speed trials. Specifying the object of a's intention to indicate to b that he in on speed trials requires a specification of these two intended references. The intention to indicate to b that he is on speed trials and the intention to indicate to c that he is on speed trials are alike in that in both a intends to refer to the property of being on speed trials, but they differ with respect to other intended references — in the first a intends to refer to b whereas in the second intention he intends to refer to c. The notion of reference is thus required in the specification of the structure of intentions to indicate that something is the case. It is, therefore, for a good reason that we often have an intended reference in mind when we speak of meaning or a meaning.

Applying an intention to indicate is often but by no means always a verbal matter. Consider a story of Samuel Butler's about the secret life of the wife of Dr. Bentley of Trinity College, Cambridge. (See Butler (1908, pp. 201—4).) An extract from the story is made in Gardiner (1932), a work which deserves more attention than it has received hitherto in the theory of speech and language.) Mrs. Bentley, it seems, had a liking for a more than occasional tankard of beer but was shy of admitting this. To secure beer she would send her servant with her snuff-box, instead of a verbal or written order, to the college buttery. When the snuff-box was sent she got her beer, and when the snuff-box was not sent she did not get beer from the buttery. By having the servant take the snuff-box to the buttery Mrs. Bentley indicated to the butler, the tapster, that she expected him to deliver the beer. That is to say, the meaning of her action, on any one occasion of sending the servant with the snuff-box, was that she expected the butler to deliver beer.

To understand a meaning is to understand an intention to indicate that something is the case and, minimally, to understand an intention to make a reference. To understand an action with a meaning, or the meaning of an action, is to understand it as the action of an agent who makes his action conform to such an intention. Since understanding an intention to indicate is a matter of understanding an intention, it follows that understanding a meaning, or an action with a meaning, is a species of our general category of understanding intentions and intentional actions. And, of course, it may similarly be said that knowledge of meaning is a species of the general category of knowledge of facts and, more precisely, of the category of knowledge of intentions and intentional actions.

As regards the claims just made, the reader will be aware of one complication in the case of indication by verbal means. We naturally distinguish between what a speaker intends to indicate or refer to by the use of words or other linguistic elements and what these elements themselves mean. (In Jones (forthcoming) there is a comprehensive discussion of this distinction and related matters in which the tools and techniques of modal logic are used.)

Understanding a meaning, thought of as a feature of words, is also, we would wish to claim, to be able to classify certain elements as positive or negative instances of a property or relation. Briefly, this is so because the use of words is subject to norms and must be subject to norms if indication by verbal means is to be a reliable mode of communication. To use a word is to produce tokens of it; a rule for the use of a word is, therefore, a rule for the production of tokens of a certain type. For example, the rule for the use of 'you' in English is that tokens of it should be produced to refer to the listener. To say that this is the rule is to say that a reference is made to the listener in a *correct* production of a token of the word or, *equivalently* but more concisely, that the meaning of the word is the listener. To understand the meaning of the word, to know the rule, is to be able to classify productions of tokens of the word as positive or negative instances of correct use. (This, incidentally, is clearly different from the ability to state the rule.) On these grounds we think that understanding and knowledge of meanings of words are essentially like understanding and knowledge of other matters.

54. ESSENTIAL EXPLANATIONS

All explanations are answers to questions, i.e. to requests for information. Essential explanations are answers to what-questions and as such they supply information about the kind of instance some element or sequence of elements is (cf. Levison and Thalberg (1969), p. 92). Essential explanations are therefore closely connected with understanding. Something is given, for example a geometrical figure. A pupil does not know what it is, i.e. what kind of thing it is; he cannot classify it. A teacher helps him by making it clear that the figure is a triangle. In so doing the teacher exercises his understanding of triangles, supplies the pupil with the information that the figure is a triangle, and aids the pupil's acquisition of understanding of triangles. Generally speaking, in an essential explanation an agent supplies the information that a given sequence satisfies a relation and aids the acquisition of another agent's understanding of the relation which the sequence typifies.

There is room for a generalization here. Suppose the pupil asks, not for a specification of the kind of figure the instance before him is, but what kind of figure a triangle is. And suppose the teacher explains by saying that a triangle is a three-sided polygon. The teacher explains the property of being a triangle by defining it, or by using a received definition of a triangle, as the intersection of two properties, being a polygon and having three sides. In this case the teacher supplies the information that a property equals the intersection of two properties. It may also be said that the teacher states the conditions that are necessary and sufficient for something being a triangle. This kind of explanation may, perhaps, be regarded as an ideal for the essential explanation of a type in terms of one or more other types, but it would not be realistic to entertain it for all such essential explanations. It is hardly realistic to attempt to define a chair, say, in terms of necessary and sufficient conditions; the paradigm technique is preferable here.

We now return to Butler's story about Mrs. Bentley. Many essential explanations of Mrs. Bentley's action are possible relative to the possible information of the questioner. Here are some possible essential explanations of her action in relation to the servant: she intentionally gives her snuff-box to the servant; she inconveniences the servant; she intentionally addresses the servant in English; she intentionally orders the servant to deliver the snuff-box to the college buttery; she addresses the servant in English with the intention of ordering him to take the snuff-box to the buttery; she orders the servant to take the snuff-box to the buttery with the intention of ordering some beer. And here are some possible essential explanations of Mrs. Bentley's action in relation to the tapster: she intentionally sees to it that her snuff-box is sent to the tapster; she intentionally orders the tapster to deliver some beer; she has her snuff-box sent to the tapster with the intention of ordering him to deliver some beer; she has her snuff-box sent to the tapster with the intention of being discreet. Both lists could easily be made considerably longer.

In each case the explanation makes clear what kind of instance an element or sequence of elements is: in relation to the servant her action is an instance of the action (type) of inconveniencing somebody, of the action (type) of intentionally giving her snuff-box to somebody, and so forth. It is absolutely plain that such a classification must first be made if we are to go on to give an explanation of some other kind of Mrs. Bentley's action, say a causal explanation. When we explain an instance causally it is already understood or essentially explained as an instance of a definite type or relation. The causal question 'Why did she intentionally order the servant to deliver her snuff-box to the college buttery?' may be reformulated as the question 'Why is her action in relation to the servant an instance of the action (type) of intentionally ordering somebody to take her snuff-box to the college buttery?' and it can, therefore, readily be seen that the causal question presupposes that the type of the instance to be explained has been identified.

The why-question cannot be answered in terms of the intention to order the servant to take the snuff-box to the buttery because this intention and knowledge of it is presupposed in the question itself. If a genuine explanation of the instance is to be given, in answer to the why-question, we must refer to factors not already relied on in the classification of the instance, for example Mrs. Bentley's intention to order some beer. However, before we pursue these matters further we must give an account of causal explanations.

55. COUNTERFACTUALS AND CAUSAL EXPLANATIONS

Essential explanations yield understanding and causal explanations yield knowledge of facts. Essential explanations are answers to what-questions, causal explanations answers to why-questions, to questions why a fact, which is known to obtain, obtains. In this section we discuss causal explanations in general in terms of a counterfactual analysis of causation. In the following section we discuss causal explanation of actions. After an interlude in Section 57 on functional explanation we go on in Section 58 to discuss explanations of actions which we do not count as causal, though they are answers to why-questions. We call explanations which are answers to why-questions connective explanations and count causal explanations as a sub-category of connective explanations.

According to Lewis (1975), a counterfactual conditional of the form 'If it were the case that p, it would be the case that q', symbolized as $p \square \rightarrow q$, is true at the actual world u if and only if either there are no possible p-worlds, i.e. no worlds in which p is true, in which case the conditional is vacuously true; or some p-world in which q is also true is closer (more similar) to u than any p-world in which q is false. Thus, when the conditional is non-vacuously true it takes less of a departure from actuality to make $(p \& q)$ true than it does to make $(p \& \sim q)$ true.

The relation of comparative similarity, which is used in the formulation of the truth condition of $p \square \rightarrow q$, is primitive in Lewis's account. It is assumed to be a complete weak ordering of possible worlds which may be indifferent to some distinct pair u, v of worlds in the sense that u may bear the ordering relation to v and at the same time v may bear it to u; and, secondly, in the ordering the actual world is assumed to be closest to actuality, i.e. it is more similar to itself than any other world.

If $p_1, p_2, ...$ is a family of mutually exclusive propositions and $q_1, q_2, ...$ another such family of the same size, then the q's depend counterfactually on the p's if and only if the counterfactuals $p_i \square \rightarrow q_i$ $(i = 1, 2, ...)$ are all true. If $p(c_i)$ is the proposition that a possible event c_i occurs and $p(e_i)$ the proposition that a possible event e_i occurs, then the family $e_1, e_2, ...$ of events depends causally on the family $c_1, c_2, ...$ of events if and only if the family $p(e_1), p(e_2), ...$ depends counterfactually on the family $p(c_1), p(c_2), ...$ And, in the limiting case, if c and e are two possible particular events, then e is said to depend causally on c if and only if the family $p(e), \sim p(e)$ depends counterfactually on the family $p(c), \sim p(c)$, in which case the counterfactuals

(1) $p(c) \square \rightarrow p(e)$

and

(2) $\sim p(c) \square \rightarrow \sim p(e)$

are both true.

It follows from Lewis's account, first, that if c and e are actual events then, because $p(c)$ and $p(e)$ imply (1), e depends causally on c if and only if (2) is true; and, secondly, that if c and e do not occur then, because $\sim p(c)$ and $\sim p(e)$ imply (2), e depends causally on c if and only if (1) is true. If $e_1, e_2, e_3, ...$ are actual events and e_2 depends causally on e_1, e_3 on e_2, and so on, then the sequence $e_1, e_2, e_3, ...$ is a causal chain. In terms of the notion of a causal chain causation may be defined as follows: an actual event c is a cause of an actual event e if and only if there is a causal chain from c to e. Thus far Lewis on counterfactual dependence, causal dependence, and causation.

According to Kim (1975), the dependence expressed by counterfactuals is not necessarily causal. For example, the counterfactual

(3)   If yesterday had not been Monday, today would not be Tuesday

is true, but should we say on the ground of this truth that today's being

Tuesday was caused by yesterday's being Monday? Similarly, the counter-factual

(4)   If George had not been born in 1950, he would not have reached the age of 21 in 1971

is true, but are we prepared to say that the fact that George reached the age of 21 in 1971 was caused by the fact that he was born in 1950? Or again, if the counterfactual

(5)   If I had not turned the knob, I would not have opened the window

is true in a situation in which

(6)   I open the window by turning the knob

is also true, then, according to Kim, the action of turning the knob does not cause the action of opening the window.

Lewis's analysis of causation is attractive, but it must also be admitted that Kim's criticism has considerable force. So we are here faced with a dilemma. We devote the balance of the present section to a brief discussion of this dilemma.

As is customary, we divide a connective explanation into two main components, the statement of the explanandum and the statement of the explanans. The statement of the explanandum does not logically or analytically imply any component of the statement of the explanans (cf. Carney and Scheer (1974), p. 392). 'p because p' or 'p because p & q' cannot, therefore, be patterns of connective explanations. This is an immediate consequence of the fact that connective explanations are answers to why-questions; supplying the information that p in reply to the question why it is the case that p does not answer the question and constitutes a pseudo-explanation. For example, supplying the information that George is an unmarried man in reply to the question why he is a bachelor does not answer the question for the obvious reason that George is a bachelor if and only if George is an unmarried man, and the question, differently put, is why George is an unmarried man. It is irrelevant here to make the point that the questioner might not know that the property of being a bachelor and the property of being an unmarried man are equal, for what is needed, then, is an essential explanation of bachelorhood; nothing but confusion results if we fail to make or otherwise blur the distinction between essential and connective explanations.

It may similarly be said that an explanatory account which exhibits the fact that George was born in 1950 as a cause of his reaching the age of 21 in 1971, is a pseudo-explanation. It, too, violates the basic requirement that the statement of the explanandum should not logically or analytically imply the statement of the explanans. The same remark applies to the account according to which today's being Tuesday is caused by yesterday's being Monday. And it applies, with one important proviso, to the account according to which an agent's opening a window is caused by his turning a knob; the proviso is that his action in relation to the knob be identified or essentially explained as an instance of opening the window by turning the knob.

On the ground of these observations on the nature of connective explanations we feel inclined to accept Lewis's counterfactual analysis of causal dependence. But the same observations make it evident that we must recognize that not all statements of causal dependence can be made to serve explanatory purposes — that some such statements are bound to yield pseudo-explanations because whenever they are made to appear in an explanatory causal account this fails to meet the general criteria of what counts as a connective explanation because of the nature of those statements. *Analytic* statements of causal dependence are useless — only true synthetic statements of causal dependence may serve for explanatory purposes. (For a lucid and most penetrating account of analyticity, see Stenius (1965).)

This way of resolving the dilemma before us obviously ignores Kim's contention that the dependence expressed by a true counterfactual is not necessarily causal. The alternative way of resolving the dilemma takes this contention seriously. The way we have in mind is to solve the characterization problem for relationships of causal dependence by stipulating, in the spirit of Hume, that all and only synthetic counterfactuals be regarded as statements of relationships of causal dependence. For example, though (3) expresses a dependence of a sort, it does not, according to the proposed criterion, express a relationship of causal dependence. This way of resolving the dilemma gives a much narrower notion of causal dependence than the first. However, the differences between the two ways, as regards causal explanation, are immaterial. According to the first way of looking at the matter, the use of (3) to explain today's being Tuesday as due to yesterday's being Monday, is a pseudo-explanation because in a genuine connective explanation the explanandum does not imply the explanans and in this case it does. According to the second point of view, the explanation is not causal because it does not employ a causal counterfactual (and it is in any case not an acceptable connective explanation because the explanandum implies the explanans). If the two approaches issue in the same verdict as to what is to count as an acceptable causal explanation, why make the choice between them a *casus belli*?

56. COUNTERFACTUALS AND EXPLANATION OF ACTIONS

According to our analysis in Section 17, a brings p about with the intention of bringing q about if and only if (i) a brings it about that p on the ground of his intention to bring it about that p and (ii) a intends to bring it about that p because a intends to bring it about that q. We now look at some possible causal explanations of elements of this volition-cognition-action complex and we begin with factor (i).

According to our analysis the formula

$$(7) \qquad B_a \text{ Shall } E_a p$$

says that a intends, unconditionally, to bring it about that p. In the terminology introduced in Section 15 the formula

$$(8) \qquad E_a(B_a \text{ Shall } E_a p \supset E_a p)$$

says that a sets himself to bring it about that p on the condition that he intends to bring it about that p. If (7) and (8) are both true, we said that a brings p about on the ground of his intention to do so or, equivalently, that he makes his action conform to his intention to bring p about. According to our conception a's action of intentionally bringing p about is the complex represented by the conjunction of (7) and (8).

Suppose now that (7) and (8) and, hence,

$$(9) \qquad E_a p$$

are true. It might be that but for his intention to bring p about a would not have set himself to bring p about on the condition that he intends to bring p about, i.e. the action expressed by (8) might depend causally on the intention expressed by (7). If so, the latter is a cause of the former. Also, the action expressed by (9) might depend causally on that expressed by (8). If so, it would follow, because causation is transitive, that the intention expressed by (7) is a cause of the action expressed by (9). But it would not follow that the latter depends causally on the former since the agent might have brought p about on some other ground (cf. Lewis (1975), p. 187).

(7) and (8) are logically independent of each other. Therefore, if we have not used the intention expressed by (7) in an essential explanation of the action expressed by (8), and if that intention is a cause of this action, we are free to give a causal explanation of the action by reference to the intention. If, on the other hand, we have referred to (8) in an essential explanation of (7), we can still give the causal explanation just mentioned, but if the infor-

mation that the explanans occurs is not based on any other evidence than the evidence on which the information that the explanandum occurs is based, our explanation must in this case be merely *ad hoc* and therefore unsatisfactory (cf. Carney and Scheer (1974), p. 395).

Similarly, (8) and (9) are logically independent of each other. So if we have not used the action expressed by (8) in an essential explanation of that expressed by (9), and if the former is a cause of the latter, we are free to use this fact to explain the second action causally by referring to the first action. With parallel provisos we may causally explain the action expressed by (9) by referring to the intention expressed by (7).

Giving a causal explanation of a's action of intentionally bringing p about is different. a could not have made his action conform to his intention to bring p about, had he not had this intention. It is true, therefore, that he would not have made his action conform to the intention, had he not had the intention. So the intention caused a's action of intentionally bringing p about. However, we cannot now use this fact to give a causal *explanation* of a's action; it is pointless to supply the information that a intended to bring p about in answer to the question of why a brought p about intentionally. Reference to the intention belongs in the essential explanation of a's action as an instance of bringing p about intentionally.

In order to understand causal explanations of a's action of intentionally bringing p about we have to turn to factor (ii) of the volition-cognition-action complex which makes up an action of doing something with the intention of doing another. But, obviously, the same general considerations apply as those we have just adduced in connection with factor (i). Unless we have relied on a's intention to bring p about in our essential explanation of his intention to bring q about, the latter may be used in a causal explanation of the former, provided of course that the truth of the relevant counterfactuals is forthcoming. This is so both in the case of derivation and in the case of evolvement of intentions. The causal dependence of intentions on beliefs concerning means is entirely similar. For illustrations we return once more to Butler's story about Mrs. Bentley. Her action in relation to the servant has been essentially explained, we assume, as an instance of intentionally ordering the servant to take her snuff-box to the college buttery. If we wish to give a causal explanation of her action, in terms of intentions or other beliefs, we must ascertain the truth values of statements such as the following: if Mrs. Bentley had not intended to order some beer from the buttery, she would not also have intended to order the servant to take the snuff-box to the buttery; if she had not believed that ordering the servant to take the snuff-box to the buttery was a means of ordering beer from the buttery in a discreet way, she would not have intended to order the servant; if she had not intended to obtain some beer from the buttery, she would not have ordered beer from the buttery; if she had not believed that ordering beer from the buttery was a means of obtaining beer, she would not have ordered beer from the buttery; and so forth. If these statements, among others, are true, there exists a definite network of relationships of causal dependence and, *a fortiori*, a definite system of causal chains. It is not possible within this system to explain Mrs. Bentley's action causally in terms of the intention which partly defines the action. This, however, does not preclude a causal explanation of the action. Since the action is caused by the intention, we may give a causal explanation of the action in terms of other intentions and beliefs in a causal chain which has the action as its ultimate member and the intention to do the action as its penultimate member.

Consider, finally, Mrs. Bentley's intention to drink the beer she so artfully secured and consider it under the assumption that she had a desire to drink the beer and intended to drink it for that reason, in the language of L:

(10) $\quad (B_a \text{ Ought } E_a p \ \& \ B_a(\text{Ought } E_a p \supset \text{Shall } E_a p)).$

Suppose also that she would not have intended to drink without the thirst or without the intention to drink if thirsty. Then her unconditional intention to drink was caused by the thirst and the intention to drink if thirsty.

57. FUNCTIONAL EXPLANATION

In the study of dynamic systems functional explanations occur frequently. The nature of such explanations has attracted attention in the methodology of social science and especially in the methodology of anthropology. Here we shall briefly consider two examples of functional explanation not only in order to illustrate a conception of functional explanation but also and primarily in order to prevent a possible misunderstanding about essential and connective explanations.

A gravity hot water circulation system is operated by heating water in a boiler. As the water is heated, it expands a little and its density is slightly reduced. This gives it a tendency to rise to the top of the system, changing places with cooler and therefore heavier water, which sinks to the bottom of the boiler, where it is reheated and rises again. At the top of the system there is a so-called expansion tank. Suppose now that we essentially explain the tank in the following way. The tank collects the excess volume of water created by the heating of the water in the system. The fact that the tank collects the excess volume causes the system not to burst. In other words, the expansion tank is a reservoir which stops the heated and expanded water from bursting the system. This is what an expansion tank is (like).

An important element in this *essential* explanation is the statement of a causal relationship. In giving the essential explanation of the tank as the expansion tank of the hot water system we refer to and rely on the fact that the tank causes the system not to burst. There is nothing in our account of essential and connective explanations, especially connective explanations of the causal variety, which prevents a statement of a causal relationship to be used in the way illustrated in an essential explanation. It is plain, or so it seems to us, that at least some so-called functional explanations are essential explanations, and one idea would be to define a functional explanation as an explanation in which it is made clear what an instance is by exhibiting it, or a fact about it, as a term of a causal relationship; or in which a type is defined as the type of instances so identified. If this idea is accepted, functional explanations will constitute a subcategory of essential explanations. It is sometimes said, by way of criticism, that functional explanations fail to meet minimal requirements of an adequate explanation. If this is taken to mean that they fail to meet minimal requirements of causal or, more generally, connective explanations, and if the suggestion we just made about functional explanations is correct, the criticism is clearly mistaken because it is predicated on a mistaken assumption about the nature of a functional explanation.

In the above example, in which a tank is explained essentially, or functionally, as the reservoir which stops a hot water system from bursting a fact about the tank is exhibited as a cause of another fact. It is easy to find examples of functional explanation in which an instance is essentially explained by exhibiting it as the effect of a certain cause. Suppose we wish to give a functional explanation of a ceremony in an attempt to distinguish between, say, the plain disposal of a dead human body and a funeral thought of as a ceremonious disposal of a body. And suppose that we explain that a funeral is a disposal of a dead human body which is governed in detail by an organization and, secondly, that the proceeding is so organized because the participants intend to express certain feeling-states. Suppose, in other words, that a funeral is explained as a disposal of a body which is organized with the intention, usually shared by several participant agents, of expressing certain feeling-states. On the assumption that the intention to express certain feeling-states causes the participants to organize the disposal of the body in the way they do, we would, then, have given an essential explanation of a funeral by exhibiting it, *qua* a proceeding, as the effect of a certain intention as a cause. And on the assumption that our tentative hypothesis about functional explanations is correct, we would have given a functional explanation of a funeral.

58. LAWS AND EXPLANATION OF ACTIONS

In Section 45 we considered a simple dynamic action system: an agent regulates the distance between two objects X and Y by moving X along a line F, his goal is to keep the interval XY at 100 units, and his policy is to correct the inventory error at the rate of one-tenth of the error per second. We saw that it is possible, on the basis of the assumptions we made, and given an arbitrary state of the system, to determine uniquely the next state of the system. This is possible because the system is subject to a *law*. The law is that the relation between the state of the system and its rate of change at any moment remains the same.

We have here an example of the kind of invariable relation which the scientific man seeks in his search for order among facts. A comparable example would be the principle of the lever, which states that equilibrium is obtained when the two weights vary inversely to their distance from the fulcrum or, better still, Galileo's law of freely falling bodies, which says that the acceleration of a freely falling body, defined as the change in velocity during any unit of time, is constant and 32 feet per second. In the latter case the law is that the relation between the state of a system, which comprises a body in free fall towards the Earth, and the rate of change of the state at any moment is invariable (cf. Stenius (1975), pp. 96–8 and pp. 187–9). The law, therefore, allows us to determine the successor of every state of the system.

The situation is the same in the case of our sample system of dynamic action. Let p_i be a true proposition of the state of the system at a given moment and q_i, $i = 1, 2, ...$, a true proposition of the state of the system at the next moment. That the dynamic law allows us to determine the successor of any state means that we can *deduce* the conditionals $(p_i \supset q_i)$ from the law. In other words, the law is such that it implies that *if* the system at a given time is in a state s, *then* it is in state s' at the next moment. Following Lewis (1975, p. 187), we shall say that the family $q_1, q_2, ...$ depends nomically on the family $p_1, p_2, ...$ if and only if there is a nonempty set $\mathscr{L}$ of true law-propositions and a set $\mathscr{F}$ of true propositions of particular fact such that $\mathscr{L}$ and $\mathscr{F}$ jointly imply, but $\mathscr{F}$ alone does not imply, the material conditionals $(p_i \supset q_i)$, $i = 1, 2, ...$ If there is a nomic dependence it is said to hold in virtue of $\mathscr{L}$ and $\mathscr{F}$. In our example $\mathscr{F}$ is empty and the nomic dependence of the q's on the p's thus holds in virtue of the dynamic law alone.

Nomic dependence does not imply counterfactual dependence. Lewis (1975, p. 188) shows that nomic dependence implies counterfactual dependence if and only if the further condition that all members of $\mathscr{L}$ and $\mathscr{F}$ be counterfactually independent of the p's is fulfilled. In our sample system the nomic dependence does not imply the corresponding counterfactual dependence. This is so because, as we have set up the example, the p's make a reference to, for instance, the implementation of the policy of correcting the inventory error at a certain rate; if the agent were to change the policy, the law might not, and probably would not, hold any longer, in which case it is not counterfactually independent of the p's.

Since nomic dependence does not imply counterfactual dependence, it would be misleading, from the point of view of a Lewis-style analysis of causal dependence and causation, to call every dynamic law of the kind now under consideration a dynamic causal law. This expression is best reserved for dynamic laws which sustain counterfactual conditionals in the sense that the nomic dependence which holds in virtue of the laws does imply the corresponding counterfactual dependence.

Nomic dependence, whether or not it implies counterfactual dependence, may be used for explanatory purposes. To say that our sample system is now in state s' because it was in state s at the previous moment and because the system changes at such and such a rate, is to give a connective explanation because it answers or would answer the question why the system is in state s' at the present moment. However, in view of what was said above, it is clear that not all connective explanations which employ statements of nomic dependence in this way are causal explanations.

59. FREE WILL AND THE VALIDITY OF LAWS

The objection might be raised that the likeness between the law of our sample dynamic action system and, say, Galileo's law of freely falling bodies is not as complete as we have tried to make it out to be. Is there not, it might be asked, an enormous difference between the two cases? The axiom of free will applies to the agent in our action system. That is to say, this agent can act contrary to any prediction of his action that is made on the basis of the dynamic law or, in other words, the agent can suspend the law, cause it to cease to be valid. But, on the other hand, a body that is falling freely towards the Earth has no such power. Should no weight be given to this difference?

We would wish to maintain that the difference does not amount to a difference between the two laws as such. In the case of our sample system the rate of change is constant, and on the basis of this law we can determine every state of the system by proceeding from an initial state as long as the agent in his action continues to act in accordance with the law. In the case of Galileo's law, the acceleration of a freely falling body − a rate of change − is constant. On the basis of the law we can compute every state of a system which comprises a freely falling body by proceeding from an initial state, and we can do this as long as the body continues to follow the law in its motion. Thus far the two cases are entirely parallel; both laws are propensity laws.

The difference mentioned above is relevant, not to the status of these invariant relations as laws, but to the different issue of why the laws are valid. After Newton we answer this question for the law of uniformly accelerated motion by deriving it from the universal law of gravitation. In the case of our sample system we answer the question by explaining why the agent has adopted the policy he is pursuing. This is an action-explanation in contradistinction to the explanation of Galileo's law. There is a tendency in the philosophy of social science to think that a law cannot be genuine, if it is within the power of an agent to cause the law to cease to hold. But why? Is it because the law is likely to have a temporally restricted validity? If so, we suggest that the tendency is based on a misconception about the invariability that is characteristic of laws; this is not the same as permanence in time.

60. Agents

In this work we have frequently referred to agents, to individuals who can act in relation to themselves and other individuals. Some of the time we have made and relied on no assumptions about agents. And some of the time we have clearly intended a reference to agents with specific properties − for example agents who are also human, or agents who are also persons, or agents to whom the axiom of rationality and the axiom of free will apply. There are many fascinating philosophical questions concerning the interrelations of such species or groups of agents and many questions concerning the role one might give to agency in the explication of such notions as those of a person, a human being, an animal, or a rational animal. Few of them are easily understood or answered. To go on now to discuss these enigmas would disrupt the economy of this work and make its frame crumble under the strain. This is, therefore, a suitable place for letting the work come to an end.

BIBLIOGRAPHY

Anderson, A. R., *The Formal Analysis of Normative Systems*, New Haven: Interaction Laboratory, Yale University, 1956; reprinted in Rescher, N. (ed.), *The Logic of Decision and Action*, University of Pittsburgh Press, Pittsburgh, 1967.

Bonacich, P., 'Putting the Dilemma Back into Prisoner's Dilemma', *Journal of Conflict Resolution* 14 (1970), 379–87.

Buckley, W. (ed.), *Modern Systems Research for the Behavioral Scientist*, Aldine Publishing Company, Chicago, 1968.

Butler, S., *Essays of Life, Art, and Science*, (ed. by Streatfeild, R. A.), Fifield, London, 1908.

Carney, J. D. and Scheer, R. K., *Fundamentals of Logic*, 2nd edition, Macmillan Publishing Co., Inc., New York, 1974.

Chapple, E. L. and Coon, C. S., *Principles of Anthropology*, Jonathan Cape, London, 1947.

Chellas, B. F., *The Logical Form of Imperatives*, Perry Lane Press, Stanford, California, 1969.

Chisholm, R. M., 'Epistemic Statements and the Ethics of Belief', *Philosophy and Phenomenological Research* 16 (1955–56), 447–60.

Fishbein, M., 'A Consideration of Beliefs, Attitudes and their Relationships', in Steiner, I. D. and Fishbein, M. (eds.), *Current Studies in Social Psychology*, Holt, Rinehart and Winston Ltd., London, 1965.

Fishbein, M., 'The Relationship between Beliefs, Attitudes and Behaviour', in Feldman, S. (ed.), *Cognitive Consistency*, Academic Press, London, 1966.

Forrester, J. W., *Industrial Dynamics*, The M.I.T. Press, Cambridge, Massachusetts, 1961.

Forrester, J. W., *Principles of Systems*, Wright-Allen Press, Cambridge, Massachusetts, 1968.

Gardiner, A., *The Theory of Speech and Language*, The Clarendon Press, Oxford, 1932.

Goldman, A. I., *A Theory of Human Action*, Prentice-Hall, Inc., Englewood Cliffs, New Jersey, 1970.

Harary, F., 'Graph Theoretic Methods in the Management Sciences', *Management Science* 5 (1959), 387–403; reprinted in Luce, Bush and Galanter (1965) under the title 'Graph Theory and Group Structure'.

Hayek, F. A., *Studies in Philosophy, Politics and Society*, Routledge & Kegan Paul Ltd., London, 1967.

Hilpinen, R., 'On the Semantics of Personal Directives', *Ajatus* 35 (1973).

Homans, G. C., *The Human Group*, Routledge & Kegan Paul Ltd., London, 1951.

Howard, N., 'The Theory of Meta-Games', *General Systems* 11 (1966a), 167–186.

Howard, N., 'The Mathematics of Meta-Games', *General Systems* 11 (1966b), 187–200.

Jones, A. J. I., *Communication and Meaning. An Essay in Applied Modal Logic*, forthcoming.

Kanger, S., 'Law and Logic', *Theoria* 38 (1972), 105–132.

Kanger, S. and Kanger, H., 'Rights and Parliamentarism', *Theoria* 32 (1966), 85–115.

Kelvin, P., *The Bases of Social Behaviour*, Holt, Rinehart and Winston Ltd., London, 1969.

Kemeny, J. G., Snell, J. L. and Thompson, G. L., *Introduction to Finite Mathematics*, Prentice-Hall, Inc., Englewood Cliffs, New Jersey, 1964.

Kim, J., 'Causes and Counterfactuals', *Journal of Philosophy* 70 (1973), 570–2; reprinted in Sosa, E. (ed.), *Causation and Conditionals*, Oxford University Press, Oxford, 1975.

Levison, A. B. and Thalberg, I., 'Essential and Causal Explanations of Action', *Mind* 78 (1969), 91–101.
Lewis, D., 'Causation', *Journal of Philosophy* 70 (1973), 556–67; reprinted in Sosa, E. (ed.), *Causation and Conditionals*, Oxford University Press, Oxford, 1975.
Lindahl, L., *Position and Change*, D. Reidel Publishing Company, Dordrecht, 1977.
Lindenmayer, A., 'Mathematical Models for Cellular Interactions in Development', *Journal of Theoretical Biology* 18 (1968), I: 280–299; II: 300–315.
Lindenmayer, A., 'Developmental Systems without Cellular Interactions, their Languages and Grammars', *Journal of Theoretical Biology* 30 (1971), 455–484.
Luce, R. D., 'Connectivity and Generalized Cliques in Sociometric Group Structures', *Psychometrika* 15 (1950), 169–190.
Luce, R. D., Bush, R. R. and Galanter, E. (eds.), *Readings in Mathematical Psychology*, vol. II, John Wiley & Sons, Inc., New York, 1965.
MacKay, D. M., 'Towards an Information-Flow Model of Human Behaviour', *British Journal of Psychology* 47 (1956), 30–43; reprinted in Buckley (1968).
Needham, P., *A Semantic Approach to Causal Logic*, M. A. thesis deposited in Birmingham University Library, 1971.
Nietzsche, F., *The Will to Power* (Transl. by W. Kaufman), Vintage Books, New York, 1968.
Nordenfelt, L., *Explanation of Human Actions*, Department of Philosophy, University of Uppsala, Uppsala, 1974.
Nurmi, H., 'Ways Out of the Prisoner's Dilemma', *Proceedings of the VIth General Conference of the International Peace Research Association held in Turku 1975*.
Pörn, I., *The Logic of Power*, Basil Blackwell, Oxford, 1970.
Pörn, I., *Elements of Social Analysis*, Department of Philosophy, University of Uppsala, Uppsala, 1971.
Pörn, I., 'Some Basic Concepts of Action', in Stenlund, S. (ed.), *Logical Theory and Semantic Analysis*, D. Reidel Publishing Company, Dordrecht, 1974.
Robbin, J. W., *Mathematical Logic*, W. A. Benjamin, Inc., New York, 1969.
Salomaa, A., *Theory of Automata*, Pergamon Press, London, 1969.
Salomaa, A., *Formal Languages*, Academic Press, New York, 1973.
Shapley, L. S. and Subik, M., 'A Method of Evaluating the Distribution of Power in a Committee System', *American Political Science Review* 48 (1954), 787–792.
Sommerhoff, G., 'The Abstract Characteristics of Living Systems', in Emery, F. E. (ed.), *Systems Thinking*, Penguin Books Ltd., Harmondsworth, 1969.
Stenius, E., 'Definitions of the Concept 'Value-Judgment' ', *Theoria* 21 (1955), 131–145; reprinted in Stenius (1972).
Stenius, E., 'The Definition of Analyticity', in Stenius (1972).
Stenius, E., *Critical Essays* (Acta Philosophica Fennica, Fasc. XXV.), North-Holland Publishing Company, Amsterdam, 1972.
Stenius, E., *Tankens Gryning* [*The Dawn of Thought*], 2nd edition, Söderströms, Helsingfors, 1975.
Taylor, R., *Action and Purpose*, Prentice-Hall, Inc., Englewood Cliffs, New Jersey, 1966.
Taylor, R., 'Purposeful and Non-Purposeful Behaviour: A Rejoinder', *Philosophy of Science* 17 (1950), 327–32; reprinted in Buckley (1968).
von Wright, G. H., *Explanation and Understanding*, Routledge & Kegan Paul Ltd., London, 1971.
von Wright, G. H., 'On so-called Practical Inference', *Acta Sociologica* 15 (1972), 39–53.
Walton, D., 'Modal Logic and Agency', *Logique et Analyse* 69–70 (1975), 103–11.

INDEX

act, *see also* action and agent-causality
instance, 12–3
relations, 13–4, 65
and N-equality, 13–6
their restriction to agents of a
specified type, 109
action, *see also* act and agent-causality
causal theory of, 5, 11–3
characterization problem for, 11, 18
complexes (*see also* activities and
proceedings), 43–4, 50, 78, 79, 83
consequences of, 16–7
dynamic aspects of, *see* dynamic systems and social dynamics
-explanations, *see* explanations
for a reason, 35, 54, 71, 72
in consequence relation to an agent,
76–7, 78, 91
intentional, 28–31, 35, 70–3, 87–8,
102, 104, 117
modalities
primitive (basic), 4–6
defined, 6–9, 16–7
simple, 43
theory, IX, 64
with a meaning, 110–11
activities, 43–4, 56–7
structure of, 44–5, 83
agency, *see* next entry
agent-causality, 5, 7, 123
logical features of, 8, 9, 10, 14, 15
transmission of, 48–51, 52–4, 77
agents (*see also* man as agent), 13, 123
Anderson, 27
Anscombe, 88
attitudes, 38, 40–2
automata, 44–8
as finite-state acceptors, 47
in dynamic action, 86–7, 89–90
in generation of action complexes,
46, 48–51, 52–4
Mealy, 46
Moore, 46
operation of, 45, 48, 49–50

without outputs, 46

belief (*see also* information), 18, 107
acting on the ground of a, 29–30
logical features of, 19–21, 39
Bonacich, 97
Buckley, 104
Butler, 110

'can do', *see* power
Carney, 115, 118
causal chains, 114, 116, 119
causal dependence, 114–5, 116, 117, 119
causal laws, 122
causal systems with feedback, *see* cybernetic systems
cause, 114
Chapple, 79
characterization problems, IX, 11, 18
Chellas, 7–8
Chisholm, 107
cliques, *see* social groups
coercion, 73
commitment
activation of, 72
inducement of, 72, 76
communication, 63, 73, 75, 76, 77
meta-, 101
communities, 80
control, 64
in consequence relation to an agent,
77
in relation to an agent, 65–6, 77, 78
negative, 72–3
over an agent, 68, 70–3, 76, 77, 78
positive, 72–3
potential, *see* influence
convincing, 72, 73, 74
Coon, 79
counteraction conditionality, 19–20
logical features of, 6, 7–8, 10
counterfactual conditionals, 113–4
counterfactual dependence, 114, 122
cybernetics, 83, 102, 103

SYNTHESE LIBRARY

Monographs on Epistemology, Logic, Methodology,
Philosophy of Science, Sociology of Science and of Knowledge, and on the
Mathematical Methods of Social and Behavioral Sciences

Managing Editor:
JAAKKO HINTIKKA (Academy of Finland and Stanford University)

Editors:

ROBERT S. COHEN (Boston University)
DONALD DAVIDSON (University of Chicago)
GABRIËL NUCHELMANS (University of Leyden)
WESLEY C. SALMON (University of Arizona)

1. J. M. Bocheński, *A Precis of Mathematical Logic*. 1959, X + 100 pp.
2. P. L. Guiraud, *Problèmes et méthodes de la statistique linguistique*. 1960, VI + 146 pp.
3. Hans Freudenthal (ed.), *The Concept and the Role of the Model in Mathematics and Natural and Social Sciences*, Proceedings of a Colloquium held at Utrecht, The Netherlands, January 1960. 1961, VI + 194 pp.
4. Evert W. Beth, *Formal Methods. An Introduction to Symbolic Logic and the Study of Effective Operations in Arithmetic and Logic*. 1962, XIV + 170 pp.
5. B. H. Kazemier and D. Vuysje (eds.), *Logic and Language. Studies Dedicated to Professor Rudolf Carnap on the Occasion of His Seventieth Birthday*. 1962, VI + 256 pp.
6. Marx W. Wartofsky (ed.), *Proceedings of the Boston Colloquium for the Philosophy of Science, 1961-1962*, Boston Studies in the Philosophy of Science (ed. by Robert S. Cohen and Marx W. Wartofsky), Volume I. 1973, VIII + 212 pp.
7. A. A. Zinov'ev, *Philosophical Problems of Many-Valued Logic*. 1963, XIV + 155 pp.
8. Georges Gurvitch, *The Spectrum of Social Time*. 1964, XXVI + 152 pp.
9. Paul Lorenzen, *Formal Logic*. 1965, VIII + 123 pp.
10. Robert S. Cohen and Marx W. Wartofsky (eds.), *In Honor of Philipp Frank*, Boston Studies in the Philosophy of Science (ed. by Robert S. Cohen and Marx W. Wartofsky), Volume II. 1965, XXXIV + 475 pp.
11. Evert W. Beth, *Mathematical Thought. An Introduction to the Philosophy of Mathematics*. 1965, XII + 208 pp.
12. Evert W. Beth and Jean Piaget, *Mathematical Epistemology and Psychology*. 1966, XII + 326 pp.
13. Guido Küng, *Ontology and the Logistic Analysis of Language. An Enquiry into the Contemporary Views on Universals*. 1967, XI + 210 pp.
14. Robert S. Cohen and Marx W. Wartofsky (eds.), *Proceedings of the Boston Colloquium for the Philosophy of Science 1964-1966, in Memory of Norwood Russell Hanson*, Boston Studies in the Philosophy of Science (ed. by Robert S. Cohen and Marx W. Wartofsky), Volume III. 1967, XLIX + 489 pp.

15. C. D. Broad, *Induction, Probability, and Causation. Selected Papers.* 1968, XI + 296 pp.
16. Günther Patzig, *Aristotle's Theory of the Syllogism. A Logical-Philosophical Study of Book A of the Prior Analytics.* 1968, XVII + 215 pp.
17. Nicholas Rescher, *Topics in Philosophical Logic.* 1968, XIV + 347 pp.
18. Robert S. Cohen and Marx W. Wartofsky (eds.), *Proceedings of the Boston Colloquium for the Philosophy of Science 1966-1968,* Boston Studies in the Philosophy of Science (ed. by Robert S. Cohen and Marx W. Wartofsky), Volume IV. 1969, VIII + 537 pp.
19. Robert S. Cohen and Marx W. Wartofsky (eds.), *Proceedings of the Boston Colloquium for the Philosophy of Science 1966-1968,* Boston Studies in the Philosophy of Science (ed. by Robert S. Cohen and Marx W. Wartofsky), Volume V. 1969, VIII + 482 pp.
20. J.W. Davis, D. J. Hockney, and W. K. Wilson (eds.), *Philosophical Logic.* 1969, VIII + 277 pp.
21. D. Davidson and J. Hintikka (eds.), *Words and Objections: Essays on the Work of W.V. Quine.* 1969, VIII + 366 pp.
22. Patrick Suppes, *Studies in the Methodology and Foundations of Science. Selected Papers from 1911 to 1969.* 1969, XII + 473 pp.
23. Jaakko Hintikka, *Models for Modalities. Selected Essays.* 1969, IX + 220 pp.
24. Nicholas Rescher *et al.* (eds.), *Essays in Honor of Carl G. Hempel. A Tribute on the Occasion of His Sixty-Fifth Birthday.* 1969, VII + 272 pp.
25. P. V. Tavanec (ed.), *Problems of the Logic of Scientific Knowledge.* 1969, XII + 429 pp.
26. Marshall Swain (ed.), *Induction, Acceptance, and Rational Belief.* 1970, VII + 232 pp.
27. Robert S. Cohen and Raymond J. Seeger (eds.), *Ernst Mach: Physicist and Philosopher,* Boston Studies in the Philosophy of Science (ed. by Robert S. Cohen and Marx W. Wartofsky), Volume VI. 1970, VIII + 295 pp.
28. Jaakko Hintikka and Patrick Suppes, *Information and Inference.* 1970, X + 336 pp.
29. Karel Lambert, *Philosophical Problems in Logic. Some Recent Developments.* 1970, VII + 176 pp.
30. Rolf A. Eberle, *Nominalistic Systems.* 1970, IX + 217 pp.
31. Paul Weingartner and Gerhard Zecha (eds.), *Induction, Physics, and Ethics: Proceedings and Discussions of the 1968 Salzburg Colloquium in the Philosophy of Science.* 1970, X + 382 pp.
32. Evert W. Beth, *Aspects of Modern Logic.* 1970, XI + 176 pp.
33. Risto Hilpinen (ed.), *Deontic Logic: Introductory and Systematic Readings.* 1971, VII + 182 pp.
34. Jean-Louis Krivine, *Introduction to Axiomatic Set Theory.* 1971, VII + 98 pp.
35. Joseph D. Sneed, *The Logical Structure of Mathematical Physics.* 1971, XV + 311 pp.
36. Carl R. Kordig, *The Justification of Scientific Change.* 1971, XIV + 119 pp.
37. Milič Čapek, *Bergson and Modern Physics,* Boston Studies in the Philosophy of Science (ed. by Robert S. Cohen and Marx W. Wartofsky), Volume VII. 1971, XV + 414 pp.

38. Norwood Russell Hanson, *What I Do Not Believe, and Other Essays* (ed. by Stephen Toulmin and Harry Woolf), 1971, XII + 390 pp.
39. Roger C. Buck and Robert S. Cohen (eds.), *PSA 1970. In Memory of Rudolf Carnap*, Boston Studies in the Philosophy of Science (ed. by Robert S. Cohen and Marx W. Wartofsky), Volume VIII. 1971, LXVI + 615 pp. Also available as paperback.
40. Donald Davidson and Gilbert Harman (eds.), *Semantics of Natural Language.* 1972, X + 769 pp. Also available as paperback.
41. Yehoshua Bar-Hillel (ed.), *Pragmatics of Natural Languages.* 1971, VII + 231 pp.
42. Sören Stenlund, *Combinators, λ-Terms and Proof Theory.* 1972, 184 pp.
43. Martin Strauss, *Modern Physics and Its Philosophy. Selected Papers in the Logic, History, and Philosophy of Science.* 1972, X + 297 pp.
44. Mario Bunge, *Method, Model and Matter.* 1973, VII + 196 pp.
45. Mario Bunge, *Philosophy of Physics.* 1973, IX + 248 pp.
46. A. A. Zinov'ev, *Foundations of the Logical Theory of Scientific Knowledge (Complex Logic)*, Boston Studies in the Philosophy of Science (ed. by Robert S. Cohen and Marx W. Wartofsky), Volume IX. Revised and enlarged English edition with an appendix, by G. A. Smirnov, E. A. Sidorenka, A. M. Fedina, and L. A. Bobrova. 1973, XXII + 301 pp. Also available as paperback.
47. Ladislav Tondl, *Scientific Procedures*, Boston Studies in the Philosophy of Science (ed. by Robert S. Cohen and Marx W. Wartofsky), Volume X. 1973, XII + 268 pp. Also available as paperback.
48. Norwood Russell Hanson, *Constellations and Conjectures* (ed. by Willard C. Humphreys, Jr.). 1973, X + 282 pp.
49. K. J. J. Hintikka, J. M. E. Moravcsik, and P. Suppes (eds.), *Approaches to Natural Language. Proceedings of the 1970 Stanford Workshop on Grammar and Semantics.* 1973, VIII + 526 pp. Also available as paperback.
50. Mario Bunge (ed.), *Exact Philosophy − Problems, Tools, and Goals.* 1973, X + 214 pp.
51. Radu J. Bogdan and Ilkka Niiniluoto (eds.), *Logic, Language, and Probability. A Selection of Papers Contributed to Sections IV, VI, and XI of the Fourth International Congress for Logic, Methodology, and Philosophy of Science, Bucharest, September 1971.* 1973, X + 323 pp.
52. Glenn Pearce and Patrick Maynard (eds.), *Conceptual Chance.* 1973, XII + 282 pp.
53. Ilkka Niiniluoto and Raimo Tuomela, *Theoretical Concepts and Hypothetico-Inductive Inference.* 1973, VII + 264 pp.
54. Roland Fraïssé, *Course of Mathematical Logic − Volume 1: Relation and Logical Formula.* 1973, XVI + 186 pp. Also available as paperback.
55. Adolf Grünbaum, *Philosophical Problems of Space and Time.* Second, enlarged edition, Boston Studies in the Philosophy of Science (ed. by Robert S. Cohen and Marx W. Wartofsky), Volume XII. 1973, XXIII + 884 pp. Also available as paperback.
56. Patrick Suppes (ed.), *Space, Time, and Geometry.* 1973, XI + 424 pp.
57. Hans Kelsen, *Essays in Legal and Moral Philosophy*, selected and introduced by Ota Weinberger. 1973, XXVIII + 300 pp.
58. R. J. Seeger and Robert S. Cohen (eds.), *Philosophical Foundations of Science. Proceedings of an AAAS Program, 1969*, Boston Studies in the Philosophy of

Science (ed. by Robert S. Cohen and Marx W. Wartofsky), Volume XI. 1974, X + 545 pp. Also available as paperback.

59. Robert S. Cohen and Marx W. Wartofsky (eds.), *Logical and Epistemological Studies in Contemporary Physics*, Boston Studies in the Philosophy of Science (ed. by Robert S. Cohen and Marx W. Wartofsky), Volume XIII. 1973, VIII + 462 pp. Also available as paperback.

60. Robert S. Cohen and Marx W. Wartofsky (eds.), *Methodological and Historical Essays in the Natural and Social Sciences. Proceedings of the Boston Colloquium for the Philosophy of Science, 1969-1972*, Boston Studies in the Philosophy of Science (ed. by Robert S. Cohen and Marx W. Wartofsky), Volume XIV. 1974, VIII + 405 pp. Also available as paperback.

61. Robert S. Cohen, J. J. Stachel and Marx W. Wartofsky (eds.), *For Dirk Struik. Scientific, Historical and Political Essays in Honor of Dirk J. Struik*, Boston Studies in the Philosophy of Science (ed. by Robert S. Cohen and Marx W. Wartofsky), Volume XV. 1974, XXVII + 652 pp. Also available as paperback.

62. Kazimierz Ajdukiewicz, *Pragmatic Logic*, transl. from the Polish by Olgierd Wojtasiewicz. 1974, XV + 460 pp.

63. Sören Stenlund (ed.), *Logical Theory and Semantic Analysis. Essays Dedicated to Stig Kanger on His Fiftieth Birthday*. 1974, V + 217 pp.

64. Kenneth F. Schaffner and Robert S. Cohen (eds.), *Proceedings of the 1972 Biennial Meeting, Philosophy of Science Association*, Boston Studies in the Philosophy of Science (ed. by Robert S. Cohen and Marx W. Wartofsky), Volume XX. 1974, IX + 444 pp. Also available as paperback.

65. Henry E. Kyburg, Jr., *The Logical Foundations of Statistical Inference*. 1974, IX + 421 pp.

66. Marjorie Grene, *The Understanding of Nature: Essays in the Philosophy of Biology*, Boston Studies in the Philosophy of Science (ed. by Robert S. Cohen and Marx W. Wartofsky), Volume XXIII. 1974, XII + 360 pp. Also available as paperback.

67. Jan M. Broekman, *Structuralism: Moscow, Prague, Paris*. 1974, IX + 117 pp.

68. Norman Geschwind, *Selected Papers on Language and the Brain*, Boston Studies in the Philosophy of Science (ed. by Robert S. Cohen and Marx W. Wartofsky), Volume XVI. 1974, XII + 549 pp. Also available as paperback.

69. Roland Fraïssé, *Course of Mathematical Logic – Volume 2: Model Theory*. 1974, XIX + 192 pp.

70. Andrzej Grzegorczyk, *An Outline of Mathematical Logic. Fundamental Results and Notions Explained with All Details*. 1974, X + 596 pp.

71. Franz von Kutschera, *Philosophy of Language*. 1975, VII + 305 pp.

72. Juha Manninen and Raimo Tuomela (eds.), *Essays on Explanation and Understanding. Studies in the Foundations of Humanities and Social Sciences*. 1976, VII + 440 pp.

73. Jaakko Hintikka (ed.), *Rudolf Carnap, Logical Empiricist. Materials and Perspectives*. 1975, LXVIII + 400 pp.

74. Milič Čapek (ed.), *The Concepts of Space and Time. Their Structure and Their Development*, Boston Studies in the Philosophy of Science (ed. by Robert S. Cohen and Marx W. Wartofsky), Volume XXII. 1976, LVI + 570 pp. Also available as paperback.

75. Jaakko Hintikka and Unto Remes, *The Method of Analysis. Its Geometrical Origin and Its General Significance,* Boston Studies in the Philosophy of Science (ed. by Robert S. Cohen and Marx W. Wartofsky), Volume XXV. 1974, XVIII + 144 pp. Also available as paperback.

76. John Emery Murdoch and Edith Dudley Sylla, *The Cultural Context of Medieval Learning. Proceedings of the First International Colloquium on Philosophy, Science, and Theology in the Middle Ages — September 1973,* Boston Studies in the Philosophy of Science (ed. by Robert S. Cohen and Marx W. Wartofsky), Volume XXVI. 1975, X + 566 pp. Also available as paperback.

77. Stefan Amsterdamski, *Between Experience and Metaphysics. Philosophical Problems of the Evolution of Science,* Boston Studies in the Philosophy of Science (ed. by Robert S. Cohen and Marx W. Wartofsky), Volume XXXV. 1975, XVIII + 193 pp. Also available as paperback.

78. Patrick Suppes (ed.), *Logic and Probability in Quantum Mechanics.* 1976, XV + 541 pp.

79. H. von Helmholtz, *Epistemological Writings.* (A New Selection Based upon the 1921 Volume edited by Paul Hertz and Moritz Schlick, Newly Translated and Edited by R. S. Cohen and Y. Elkana), Boston Studies in the Philosophy of Science, Volume XXXVII. 1977 (forthcoming).

80. Joseph Agassi, *Science in Flux,* Boston Studies in the Philosophy of Science (ed. by Robert S. Cohen and Marx W. Wartofsky), Volume XXVIII. 1975, XXVI + 553 pp. Also available as paperback.

81. Sandra G. Harding (ed.), *Can Theories Be Refuted? Essays on the Duhem-Quine Thesis.* 1976, XXI + 318 pp. Also available as paperback.

82. Stefan Nowak, *Methodology of Sociological Research: General Problems.* 1977, XVIII + 504 pp. (forthcoming).

83. Jean Piaget, Jean-Blaise Grize, Alina Szeminska, and Vinh Bang, *Epistemology and Psychology of Functions.* 1977 (forthcoming).

84. Marjorie Grene and Everett Mendelsohn (eds.), *Topics in the Philosophy of Biology,* Boston Studies in the Philosophy of Science (ed. by Robert S. Cohen and Marx W. Wartofsky), Volume XXVII. 1976, XIII + 454 pp. Also available as paperback.

85. E. Fischbein, *The Intuitive Sources of Probabilistic Thinking in Children.* 1975, XIII + 204 pp.

86. Ernest W. Adams, *The Logic of Conditionals. An Application of Probability to Deductive Logic.* 1975, XIII + 156 pp.

87. Marian Przełęcki and Ryszard Wójcicki (eds.), *Twenty-Five Years of Logical Methodology in Poland.* 1977, VIII + 803 pp. (forthcoming).

88. J. Topolski, *The Methodology of History.* 1976, X + 673 pp.

89. A. Kasher (ed.), *Language in Focus: Foundations, Methods and Systems. Essays Dedicated to Yehoshua Bar-Hillel,* Boston Studies in the Philosophy of Science (ed. by Robert S. Cohen and Marx W. Wartofsky), Volume XLIII. 1976, XXVIII + 679 pp. Also available as paperback.

90. Jaakko Hintikka, *The Intentions of Intentionality and Other New Models for Modalities.* 1975, XVIII + 262 pp. Also available as paperback.

91. Wolfgang Stegmüller, *Collected Papers on Epistemology, Philosophy of Science and History of Philosophy,* 2 Volumes, 1977 (forthcoming).

92. Dov M. Gabbay, *Investigations in Modal and Tense Logics with Applications to Problems in Philosophy and Linguistics.* 1976, XI + 306 pp.
93. Radu J. Bogdan, *Local Induction.* 1976, XIV + 340 pp.
94. Stefan Nowak, *Understanding and Prediction: Essays in the Methodology of Social and Behavioral Theories.* 1976, XIX + 482 pp.
95. Peter Mittelstaedt, *Philosophical Problems of Modern Physics,* Boston Studies in the Philosophy of Science (ed. by Robert S. Cohen and Marx W. Wartofsky), Volume XVIII. 1976, X + 211 pp. Also available as paperback.
96. Gerald Holton and William Blanpied (eds.), *Science and Its Public: The Changing Relationship,* Boston Studies in the Philosophy of Science (ed. by Robert S. Cohen and Marx W. Wartofsky), Volume XXXIII. 1976, XXV + 289 pp. Also available as paperback.
97. Myles Brand and Douglas Walton (eds.), *Action Theory. Proceedings of the Winnipeg Conference on Human Action, Held at Winnipeg, Manitoba, Canada, 9-11 May 1975.* 1976, VI + 345 pp.
98. Risto Hilpinen, *Knowledge and Rational Belief.* 1978 (forthcoming).
99. R. S. Cohen, P. K. Feyerabend, and M. W. Wartofsky (eds.), *Essays in Memory of Imre Lakatos,* Boston Studies in the Philosophy of Science (ed. by Robert S. Cohen and Marx W. Wartofsky), Volume XXXIX. 1976, XI + 762 pp. Also available as paperback.
100. R. S. Cohen and J. Stachel (eds.), *Leon Rosenfeld, Selected Papers.* Boston Studies in the Philosophy of Science (ed. by Robert S. Cohen and Marx W. Wartofsky), Volume XXI. 1977 (forthcoming).
101. R. S. Cohen, C. A. Hooker, A. C. Michalos, and J. W. van Evra (eds.), *PSA 1974: Proceedings of the 1974 Biennial Meeting of the Philosophy of Science Association,* Boston Studies in the Philosophy of Science (ed. by Robert S. Cohen and Marx W. Wartofsky), Volume XXXII. 1976, XIII + 734 pp. Also available as paperback.
102. Yehuda Fried and Joseph Agassi, *Paranoia: A Study in Diagnosis,* Boston Studies in the Philosophy of Science (ed. by Robert S. Cohen and Marx W. Wartofsky), Volume L. 1976, XV + 212 pp. Also available as paperback.
103. Marian Przełęcki, Klemens Szaniawski, and Ryszard Wójcicki (eds.), *Formal Methods in the Methodology of Empirical Sciences.* 1976, 455 pp.
104. John M. Vickers, *Belief and Probability.* 1976, VIII + 202 pp.
105. Kurt H. Wolff, *Surrender and Catch: Experience and Inquiry Today,* Boston Studies in the Philosophy of Science (ed. by Robert S. Cohen and Marx W. Wartofsky), Volume LI. 1976, XII + 410 pp. Also available as paperback.
106. Karel Kosík, *Dialectics of the Concrete,* Boston Studies in the Philosophy of Science (ed. by Robert S. Cohen and Marx W. Wartofsky), Volume LII. 1976, VIII + 158 pp. Also available as paperback.
107. Nelson Goodman, *The Structure of Appearance,* Boston Studies in the Philosophy of Science (ed. by Robert S. Cohen and Marx W. Wartofsky), Volume LIII. 1977 (forthcoming).
108. Jerzy Giedymin (ed.), *Kazimierz Ajdukiewicz: Scientific World-Perspective and Other Essays, 1931–1963.* 1977 (forthcoming).
109. Robert L. Causey, *Unity of Science.* 1977, VIII+185 pp.
110. Richard Grandy, *Advanced Logic for Applications.* 1977 (forthcoming).

111. Robert P. McArthur, *Tense Logic*. 1976, VII + 84 pp.
112. Lars Lindahl, *Position and Change: A Study in Law and Logic*. 1977, IX + 299 pp.
113. Raimo Tuomela, *Dispositions*. 1977 (forthcoming).
114. Herbert A. Simon, *Models of Discovery and Other Topics in the Methods of Science*, Boston Studies in the Philosophy of Science (ed. by Robert S. Cohen and Marx W. Wartofsky), Volume LIV. 1977 (forthcoming).
115. Roger D. Rosenkrantz, *Inference, Method and Decision*. 1977 (forthcoming).
116. Raimo Tuomela, *Human Action and Its Explanation. A Study on the Philosophical Foundations of Psychology*. 1977 (forthcoming).
117. Morris Lazerowitz, *The Language of Philosophy*, Boston Studies in the Philosophy of Science (ed. by Robert S. Cohen and Marx W. Wartofsky), Volume LV. 1977 (forthcoming).
118. Tran Duc Thao, *Origins of Language and Consciousness*, Boston Studies in the Philosophy of Science (ed. by Robert S. Cohen and Marx. W. Wartofsky), Volume LVI. 1977 (forthcoming).
119. Jerzy Pelc, *Polish Semiotic Studies, 1894–1969*. 1977 (forthcoming).
120. Ingmar Pörn, *Action Theory and Social Science. Some Formal Models*. 1977 (forthcoming).
121. Joseph Margolis, *Persons and Minds*, Boston Studies in the Philosophy of Science (ed. by Robert S. Cohen and Marx W. Wartofsky), Volume LVII. 1977 (forthcoming).

SYNTHESE HISTORICAL LIBRARY

Texts and Studies
in the History of Logic and Philosophy

Editors:

N. KRETZMANN (Cornell University)
G. NUCHELMANS (University of Leyden)
L. M. DE RIJK (University of Leyden)

1. M. T. Beonio-Brocchieri Fumagalli, *The Logic of Abelard.* Translated from the Italian. 1969, IX + 101 pp.
2. Gottfried Wilhelm Leibniz, *Philosophical Papers and Letters.* A selection translated and edited, with an introduction, by Leroy E. Loemker. 1969, XII + 736 pp.
3. Ernst Mally, *Logische Schriften,* ed. by Karl Wolf and Paul Weingartner. 1971, X + 340 pp.
4. Lewis White Beck (ed.), *Proceedings of the Third International Kant Congress.* 1972, XI + 718 pp.
5. Bernard Bolzano, *Theory of Science,* ed. by Jan Berg. 1973, XV + 398 pp.
6. J. M. E. Moravcsik (ed.), *Patterns in Plato's Thought. Papers Arising Out of the 1971 West Coast Greek Philosophy Conference.* 1973, VIII + 212 pp.
7. Nabil Shehaby, *The Propositional Logic of Avicenna: A Translation from al-Shifā: al-Qiyās,* with Introduction, Commentary and Glossary. 1973, XIII + 296 pp.
8. Desmond Paul Henry, *Commentary on De Grammatico: The Historical-Logical Dimensions of a Dialogue of St. Anselm's.* 1974, IX + 345 pp.
9. John Corcoran, *Ancient Logic and Its Modern Interpretations.* 1974, X + 208 pp.
10. E. M. Barth, *The Logic of the Articles in Traditional Philosophy.* 1974, XXVII + 533 pp.
11. Jaakko Hintikka, *Knowledge and the Known. Historical Perspectives in Epistemology.* 1974, XII + 243 pp.
12. E. J. Ashworth, *Language and Logic in the Post-Medieval Period.* 1974, XIII + 304 pp.
13. Aristotle, *The Nicomachean Ethics.* Translated with Commentaries and Glossary by Hypocrates G. Apostle. 1975, XXI + 372 pp.
14. R. M. Dancy, *Sense and Contradiction: A Study in Aristotle.* 1975, XII + 184 pp.
15. Wilbur Richard Knorr, *The Evolution of the Euclidean Elements. A Study of the Theory of Incommensurable Magnitudes and Its Significance for Early Greek Geometry.* 1975, IX + 374 pp.
16. Augustine, *De Dialectica.* Translated with Introduction and Notes by B. Darrell Jackson. 1975, XI + 151 pp.